MW00928628

100+ COMMON REAL ESTATE

Objections & Handling Scripts
For Real Estate Agents

Exactly What To Say To Handle 100+

Common Objections And Closing

More Deals As A Realtor

Nick Tsai &

The Soldouthouses.com's Team

SoldOutHouses.com
Your one-stop shop for real estate marketing

100+ Common Real Estate Objections & Handling
Scripts For Real Estate Agents

by Nick Tsai & The Soldouthouses.com's Team

Published by Wishstone Trading Limited

Https://soldouthouses.com

Copyright © 2022 Jaime Wishstone

All rights reserved. No portion of this book may be reproduced in any form without permission from the publisher, except as permitted by U.S. copyright law. For permissions contact: nick@soldouthouses.com

BONUSES

Thanks for getting this book; here are some resources to help you bring your real estate career to the next level.

Bonus 1- A 14 Days Free Trial Of Our Membership

You can also join our pro membership to get access to over 1700+ real estate marketing tools & templates for only a few bucks a day.

Go to https://soldouthouses.com/pro/ to try it for free.

Bonus 2- The Ultimate Real Estate Marketing Checklist

This checklist features 86 marketing tips to generate more leads online & offline.

Download your free checklist at
https://soldouthouses.com/checklist

TABLE OF CONTENTS

INTRODUCTION

Real estate is a dynamic and challenging industry where realtors often face objections from clients and customers. As a realtor, you must be prepared to address these objections to close a deal successfully. Whether you're working with buyers, sellers, or investors, objections can arise at any stage of the process.

This book has compiled a comprehensive list of 100+ common objections realtors face in the real estate industry. From pricing concerns to financing issues, we cover many objections and provide you with the exact script to handle them.

We aim to help you become more confident and effective in addressing objections and ultimately increase your success rate in closing deals. We have drawn upon the expertise of top-performing realtors and industry professionals to provide you with the most effective responses to each objection.

We understand that objections can be challenging, especially when dealing with an emotional and stressful situation. However, using our scripts, you can turn objections into opportunities and overcome any obstacle to close the deal.

Whether you're a seasoned real estate professional or just starting in the industry, this book is a valuable resource that you can refer to repeatedly. With our help, you can become a master at handling objections and take your real estate career to the next level.

ABOUT ME

Hi, I'm Nick Tsai, a digital marketing expert with over a decade of experience. Having worked as a real estate agent, I understand the challenges of generating leads and closing sales in a competitive industry. I know how it feels to put in your best efforts yet fail to see the results you desire.

When I first started, I followed the traditional advice given in the industry. However, despite my hard work, I struggled to get the desired results. It wasn't until I received an unexpected phone call from a stranger who found my blog online that I realized the power of digital marketing. That ugly little blog had become the #1 ranking real estate blog in my local area, and soon after, I began receiving more and more calls and requests for help.

Realizing the potential of digital marketing, I decided to dive deep into this field and learn everything I could about generating leads online. I studied countless books, attended seminars, and learned from the best experts in the field. I created SoldOutHouses.com as a resource for other real estate professionals who want to get results with digital marketing.

I'm excited to share my knowledge and experience with you in this comprehensive guide on handling objections in the real estate industry. I hope the insights and tips provided in this book will help you become more confident in handling objections, ultimately leading to increased success in closing deals.

To learn more about digital marketing strategies and tools for real estate professionals, visit https://SoldOutHouses.com. You can also follow our YouTube channel at https://youtube.com/@soldouthouses for more resources and insights.

Thank you for choosing this book, and I look forward to connecting with you soon.

Your one-stop shop for real estate marketing

6 EASY STEPS TO HANDLE ANY REAL ESTATE OBJECTIONS

Handling objections is essential for any successful real estate agent. It is not only about being able to convince clients or customers to accept your offer but also about addressing their concerns and building trust. This section will provide you with six easy steps to handle any real estate objections, which can help you increase your chances of closing a deal.

These six steps are based on fundamental principles of effective communication and

negotiation. By following these steps, you can create a positive and productive dialogue with your clients or customers, understand their needs and preferences, and ultimately address their concerns.

Whether you are dealing with pricing concerns, financing issues, or any other objections, these six steps can guide you through handling them effectively. We will provide you with actionable tips and strategies that you can use in your everyday work as a real estate agent.

By mastering these six steps, you can easily overcome objections, build stronger relationships with your clients or customers, and close more deals. These steps apply to any situation and can help you handle objections confidently and professionally.

So, if you are ready to take your real estate career to the next level and become an expert in handling objections, let's dive into the six easy steps to help you do just that.

1. LISTEN ATTENTIVELY TO IDENTIFY THE OBJECTION.

How often have you cut into the middle of your real estate lead's speech?

One of the essential things when handling objections is listening simply. This might sound ridiculously easy, but in reality, it's not. Yet, it's something you must do as a Realtor to achieve success, and that is handling your prospects' objections.

Why do you need to listen attentively? It's the only way for you to understand what their concerns are entirely. The less you listen, the less you know exactly what they want, and when you can't figure that out, you are already losing that prospect.

Listening to people go on about issues they know nothing about could be tedious. You're the professional and know the terms, pros, and cons, but your real estate leads don't. We understand that it may make you feel tempted to abruptly cut them short so you can share your professional expertise. Don't. Let them talk. Give them room to go on and express themselves, and you'll find out exactly what their objections are.

How do you feel when you talk to that friend or doctor who allows you to speak your mind while listening attentively? Everyone loves to be heard, and your prospects do too.

It helps them trust you more and makes them more open to the solution you'll have to give them later on. One secret tip is to write those things down in a book to help you remember them.

2. ACKNOWLEDGE THEIR QUESTIONS AND EMPATHIZE WITH THEM.

Most clients start thinking you're only there because you want to make money. They believe Realtors don't want to help them because they don't care about them. This creates a lack of trust and is detrimental to any real estate agent.

What should you do? Create that trust! One way to do it is to acknowledge the questions from your real estate lead and empathize with them.

By acknowledging or empathizing before asking clarifying questions to deal with the objection, you'll connect and be able to reframe the negative situation.

To close deals, it's important to acknowledge the concern. Hey, not by patronizing them or anything like that but with genuine acknowledgment. Here's an example;

"Moses, I understand that taking out X amount of money could prove to be daunting for you at the moment. I'd have the same concerns if I were in the same position."

Then, ask your question...

By first acknowledging the client's objection and showing empathy, you'll pave the way for your response to the sales objection, mainly because you've made the prospect realize something crucial...

You're not on opposing sides but on the same side, working together for the benefit of the prospect. It'll keep the prospect at ease and allow you to proceed.

3. ENCOURAGE QUESTIONS TO CLARIFY THE OBJECTION.

How often have you stopped short of saying everything you have in mind because you think there's no need for that?

That's how most real estate leads think too. You have listened carefully to them and let them talk, yet most won't say things exactly as they should. If you fail to find out the real problem, you may not get the sale.

What should you do in those times? Get them to talk more about that objection so that you can get a complete picture. The more the prospect talks, the more they'll reveal their concerns and the more you can address them.

For example, if a real estate prospect tells you you're too expensive, you may be urged to step in quickly and lay out all your benefits. You'll be so wrong.

Instead, you could ask a clarifying question like, "Too expensive?" In answering that question, the client will go into details concerning that objection and give you a clearer picture.

You can also ask other open-ended questions too. The goal is to get them to explain what they have in mind. Here's another thing you can do...

Lean into that objection and encourage your real estate lead by saying, "Tell me more. What's your concern; the outright expense, or the longer-term impact of the cost?"

Allow the conversation to go on so that you have more information about whether and when the deal moves forward. Handling the concern this way builds your credibility and lets the prospect know you are genuinely interested in their point of view.

Once you've asked one clarifying question or two, restate the objection for clarity's sake. For example:

"Mark, it sounds like the outright expense for this deal is something you feel you may not be able to afford at this time, especially since you've not been able to sell your property. Did I hear you correctly?"

This step suggests that you understand where the prospect is coming from, showing that you're listening, which enhances your credibility. You're also implicitly getting permission to move to the next step.

4. ISOLATE THE OBJECTION.

Has someone ever told you the truth but not the whole truth? Let me tell you a secret, and I hope you won't say anything to someone else... Prospects lie, even your real estate leads.

Sometimes, they can talk about only one thing when they still have numerous concerns. Other times, they could feel you're not right for them and then find something to use as an excuse not to move forward with you.

In any case, you have to do something about it, and one way to do that is by isolating the objection so you can be sure that it's their only concern.

For example, if the prospect objects to the price, you need to know if the price is the concern if the prospect doesn't trust that the service is worth the price, or if it's the only problem.

If there are other issues, for example, you'll most likely handle the price objection, only to hear that there's something else bothering the real estate lead. In handling objections, the goal is to get closer to closing the deal with each step.

You can say something like, *"I understand that setting aside this amount of money could be a huge thing to do at the moment, but if you could get a home that perfectly fits the kind of environment where you'd love to raise your kids, would it be worth it?"*

With this question, you'll get the prospect to tell you if it's about the money or the value they expect. If it's the money, you could go on with something like this...

"Apart from the cost of the housing, is there anything else that you'd love to talk to me about?"

Or...

"If the money wasn't the issue, is there anything else stopping you from moving forward?"

That way, you'll be isolating the objection and ensuring there are no further objections except that one. If there are others, you'll know how to handle them too.Isolate the Objection

5. ADDRESS THE CONCERN(S).

Now that you've understood the concern, it's time to act. Addressing your real estate leads' objections is vital for closing the deal. Indeed, the deal will never proceed without it, as no prospect will commit money when the concerns haven't been addressed.

This is where your expertise comes in. Knowing the problems is not enough; you must have the answer to those issues. Pro tip? Start from the most crucial objection and address it till the very last. Once you work through the most pressing barrier to moving forward, other concerns may not matter to the buyer.

Ensure you answer them in real time, as quickly, and as thoroughly as possible. The more you can do this effectively, the greater the chances of moving forward. The prospects must see why those concerns aren't problems, and you must make them see that.

Once you've responded to all the prospect's objections, verify that you've satisfied their concerns. They might have nodded during the conversation, but that doesn't mean they agreed with all that you said.

Repeat the solution and ask if they're happy with that. Explain further if need be.

Your solution must outweigh their concerns if they are to move forward. Hence, Realtors need to know how to justify their solution and help the prospect prioritize it against the others under consideration.

6. CONCLUDE AND ASK FOR THE SALE.

If you want to make a sale, you have a straightforward thing to do... Ask for that sale!

Yet, it's not as easy as it seems, as many deals fall through at this stage, leaving the Realtor frustrated and disappointed after so much effort.

When done wrong, the prospect might resort to the dreaded objection, "Let me think a little bit more about it," While this objection can be handled too, the stress is something you may want to avoid. What should you do instead?

Let the prospect ask for the sale instead. This trick is key to closing deals so easily. Here's an example...

"Since we have taken Objection A and B out of the way through this payment plan (Solution A), is there anything stopping us from moving forward?"

If you have addressed the objections well, the answer to that will be a "No," and with that, the prospect will be the one proposing that you should move forward instead of trying to do it yourself.

The step also surfaces your prospects' objections while reinforcing the progress you've made before moving to the next step.

BUYERS' OBJECTIONS

1. SPRING IS THE BEST TIME TO PURCHASE A HOUSE, SO WE WILL WAIT.

Any potential client that says this understands the seasonality of the real estate industry perfectly. In April and May, the number of houses put up for sale increases drastically, and the reason is unclear. It is probably due to the fact that people prefer to stay indoors during winter.

However, as a real estate agent, you need to convince your client why this information is half-baked genuinely, and yes, you are doing this without any selfish gain. The number of houses put up for sale increases, so the demand for houses skyrockets during spring. Home prices increase drastically, and your client might want to consider this while deciding. Winter is usually calmer. There aren't many houses, but they might also get a comfortable place at a cheaper price.

Here's a script that simulates how to tackle this common objection.

Agent: *"I understand you want to wait for spring before purchasing a house. Why do you want to do that?"*

(This will help you to know precisely what is driving your client's decision and to give your client the free will to express himself elaborately.)

Client: *"We feel spring is a better time to get a house."*

Agent: *" I can understand why you might feel that way. Spring is a popular time for people to start looking for homes, and there are often more listings on the market then. However, there are also a lot of other buyers looking at those same properties, which can make the search more competitive and drive prices up."*

On the other hand, fewer buyers are often looking for homes during the winter months, making it easier to find a property and potentially negotiate a better price. In addition, the mortgage process can take several weeks or even months, so starting the search now could give you plenty of time to get pre-approved and be ready to make an offer when you find the right property.

If you're concerned about missing out on new listings, I'd be happy to set up an automated search for you so that you'll be notified as soon as a new property that meets your criteria becomes available. That way, you can get a head start on the competition when you're ready to start looking in the spring.

Would you like me to set up that automated search for you now?"

Doing so can convince your potential client that you know your job and the person will trust you for authentic information. The client will also most likely change their decision and purchase the house.

2. WE WANT TO WAIT FOR THE MARKET TO IMPROVE.

Concerns about current events and the economy may have made the buyer wary of purchasing. You'll need to utilize your knowledge of recent economic events to allay their fears and assist them in comprehending what market conditions entail.

What most buyers fail to understand is that prices keep going higher every day. Houses keep appreciating, and it will be helpful to let your potential client know it might be the best time to get a house. It is also important to let them know that the cash depreciates in value as housing appreciates.

When a potential client informs you that they want to wait for the market to improve before commencing their house hunt, utilize this script:

Agent: *"I appreciate your desire to wait for the market to improve before beginning your property hunt. Can you tell me what you're waiting for?"*

(You want them to know that you appreciate their decision to wait, but you'd like to know why.)

Client: *"We just feel that costs are too high right now, and we want to wait for them to come down."*

Agent: *"I understand your pricing worries entirely. Real estate markets indeed fluctuate over time, and prices may alter. However, it's also crucial to remember that the market is made up of individual properties, and a variety of criteria, such as location, condition, and demand, determine the value of a given property."*

(You will only obtain a better price on the precise house you want if the market improves. Indeed, if demand for that property stays high, the price may rise.)

It's also worth noting that mortgage interest rates are now around record lows, which might make it a wise financial moment to buy. If you can discover a home that suits your wants and budget right now, it could be worth considering making an offer rather than waiting for the market to shift. However, the decision is yours, and I will be happy to help you get a good home anytime you are ready."

3. WE INTEND TO MAKE A LOW-BALL OFFER.

This is arguably the most common objection in real estate and other business transactions. The first rule is never to feel insulted or degraded. Most of the time, you might not have the answer immediately, and you might need to tell them to give you time to discuss it with your client(the seller) at the other end. This will help you approach things logically without any emotions attached.

It would help if you also discussed this with the seller. If you are already well-experienced with this objection, you can politely explain to them the repercussions of a low-ball offer and how it might be a wrong choice.

Then you need to find out why they have decided to make a low-ball offer. You can do this by strategically asking them what they think about the property's value or even asking them directly why they made such an offer. This will help you create a counter-offer, stating why the property is of more excellent value than they currently think.

16

You can also include the current market data for properties and explain to them that the current price is within normal market values.

Finally, expect a counter-offer from the buyer, and here you can negotiate with the seller if the counter-offer is favorable enough.

Here is the script that handles this:

Agent: *"I realize you want to make a low-ball offer, and I appreciate you considering me as your agent. When purchasing or selling a property, it's natural to want to receive the greatest bargain possible."*

(This is to acknowledge their decision and thank them for considering you. And also for telling you what they prefer to go with.)

Agent: *"While it is true that making a low-ball offer might occasionally result in a reduced buying price, it is also crucial to remember that it can have unforeseen repercussions. For example, the seller may reject the offer outright or counter with a higher price that is still above your desired price point. Furthermore, making a low-ball offer might harm the negotiation process and cause animosity between the buyer and seller."*

(This is to discuss the potential ramifications of making a low-ball offer; you don't have to make them forcefully comply with you, but you can definitively ensure that you are convincing enough to change their mind by giving them data-driven facts available.)

Agent: *"As your agent, I can supply you with current market data as well as advice on acceptable offer rates. This might help you decide what offer price to send while keeping your budget and goals in mind.*

I'm here to assist you through the bargaining process and achieve the greatest price possible while also taking into account the property's long-term worth."

(This is to provide market data and guidance on appropriate offer prices. This is important because now that you are done telling them the dangers of having a home at a low-ball offer, you have to give them a great alternative.)

Agent: *"Based on my market knowledge and negotiation experience, I believe I'm the best choice to help you buy or sell your home. May I get the opportunity to work with you and demonstrate my worth?"*

(This is to solicit their patronage and inform them that you are up for a deal.)

Remember to emphasize the potential consequences of making a lowball offer and offer to provide market data and guidance on appropriate offer prices. It is critical to assist the customer in making an informed selection while also considering the property's long-term worth.

4. WE ARE SEARCHING FOR A LUXURY PROPERTY EXPERT; HOW MANY HOMES WORTH OVER $1 MILLION HAVE YOU SOLD?

If you have sold homes worth more than a million dollars, you are very much good to go and answer the questions with the details of the properties you have sold and how successful it went.

If you haven't, be honest and tell them that you have not but enumerate your experience in real estate and how successful your transactions have been. Let them see your confidence and positive results; they might be convinced to transact with you.

Here is the script:

Agent: *"Thank you for inquiring about my expertise with luxury residences. Working with an agent who has the required skills and understanding to manage high-end homes is essential."*

(This is to acknowledge their inquiry, thank them for it, and appreciate them for saying what they have been thinking about since the first time they saw your listings and are willing to ask you directly.)

Agent: *"I have sold a number of luxury homes in the area, including X, Y, and Z properties. These properties cost more than $1 million and were located in XYZ communities. I have a proven track record of successfully selling luxury residences and am confident in my ability to advertise and sell them."*

(The purpose of this is to share specific instances of your experience with luxury residences; citing notable examples that are close by and are very close to the location of their property will go a long way. But If such is unavailable, you can still talk about the house you have helped build.)

Agent: *"In addition to my experience selling luxury homes, I have a deep understanding of the luxury real estate market. I remain current on the newest trends and statistics and have ties with other luxury house professionals in the region. This experience and skills, I feel, will* *be useful to you as we work together to acquire or sell your luxury house."*

(This aims to highlight your expertise in the luxury market; this is a continuation of the previous line.)

Agent: *"Based on my expertise and knowledge of the premium market, I feel I'm the greatest choice to help you purchase or sell your luxury house. May I get the opportunity to work with you and demonstrate my worth?"*

(This is to solicit their patronage and call them in to sign a contract with you.)

Remember to emphasize your relevant experience and expertise in the premium market when responding to this point. It is critical to demonstrate that you have a

Profound knowledge about how the sales of these Luxury houses go.

5. I'M RENTING A HOUSE.

The age-old topic of rent vs. own is difficult to navigate unless you understand why people prefer to rent. Is the buying process too stressful? Do they value flexibility above equity? All you will need to do is to learn as much as you can about your prospects' mindsets and respond appropriately.

Agent: *"I've seen that place, and I like it! But consider this: why pay someone else's mortgage when you can pay your own and receive an even nicer property for less money each month?"*

(This is to change their perspective about the purchase. We want to open a new conversation to help them know why they are unwilling to buy the house right now.)

Many renters believe that most mortgages cost more monthly than the average rental price. Inform your clients, and enlighten them about the potential monthly savings.

6. I'D WANT TO THINK IT OVER PROPERLY.

Most clients that do this do not end up buying the house, so it is important to help them understand it might be a regrettable objection. However, you must do that politely and try to let them realize you understand their point of view.

Here is a script to help tackle this objection.

Agent: *"I appreciate that making a large purchase, such as a home, is not something to be taken lightly. It's totally reasonable to want to think things through and make sure you're happy with your decision. I advise you to take as much time as you need to feel secure in your decision."*

(To recognize the client's apprehension and urge them to take their time as it is not a decision to rush into.)

Agent: *"If you require any extra information or resources to make a choice, please do not hesitate to ask. I am here to assist you in any way I can and to offer you all of the information you require to make an informed decision."*

(To provide more resources or information to assist them in making a decision much faster, as you already know that as happy you will be when they make their decision, they should also be delighted that they made a great decision, and not a decision that was induced by the agent on them.)

Agent: *"It's also vital to bear in mind any time-sensitive circumstances that may be at play in your selection. For example, if the house you like has many bids, it may be in your best interest to move soon. On the other side, if the property has fewer competitors, you may have more time to make a selection. I can tell you more about the present market circumstances and how they can affect your decision."*

(Remind the customer of any time-critical issues; this will help them have a great sense of urgency, which is good for them and you.)

Agent: *"I appreciate your thoughtfulness and respect your want to deliberate. Could you please let me know when you've made a choice so that I can assist you with the following steps? Whether you choose to work with me as your agent or not, I wish you the best of luck in your home hunt."*

(This is to solicit their commitment by trying to close a deal with them.)

Most clients with this objection will later have a re-think if you give them more information about the property and also let them know the property might not be on the ground before they conclude their research.

7. TEN OTHER AGENTS FROM YOUR OFFICE HAVE PHONED TODAY; I WISH YOU'D GO AWAY!

This is a call from a client who does not like follow-up or feels you are a stalker, but it is alright; we have a script that can perform the magic of getting them not to worry. Let the client understand that working with several agents might give him an edge in selling or purchasing a property. However, this must be mentioned only after you have made them realize you are not a stalker.

Agent: *"I apologize for any trouble or aggravation you have encountered due to receiving several calls from agents at my office. I realize how aggravating that might be, and I want to tell you that I am not trying to be forceful or aggressive. My major objective is to supply my customers with useful information and tools so that they may make informed decisions regarding their real estate requirements."*

(First and Foremost, this is to apologize for the inconvenience and reassure the client that you are not being aggressive.)

Agent: *"There might be several reasons why you have gotten many calls from agents at my office. Your contact information may have been shared with numerous agents, or many agents may be interested in working with you. In any event, I would be delighted to work with you to modify your contact settings and ensure that you only receive information and resources that are relevant to you. Please let me know if there is anything else I can do to improve your experience with our office."*

(This is to explain why they received many calls, propose to change their communication choices, and keep to the ones that please them.)

Agent: *"Although it may seem stressful to receive several calls from agents at my office, it is crucial to bear in mind that working with a team of agents may give many benefits. A team of agents could provide a broader outreach."*

(This is to underline the benefits of working with a team of agents and also make him aware of how beneficial it will be to work with an agent.)

This action might make you win the client's attention. The behavioral approach also matters in the handling of this objection

8. We've never heard of your firm before.

There is a widespread misconception that large corporations always do things better; for example, larger brokerages spend more money on marketing houses. While this may be accurate if all of the homes in their pipeline are counted, it is unlikely to be true regarding how much they invest in marketing individual residences.

Educate your prospects thoroughly and demonstrate that it is about the agent, not the corporation.

Here is a script that you might use to deal with the objection.

Agent: *"I understand that you are unfamiliar with our firm, and it is totally understandable that you would want to work with a company that you know and trust. Please allow me to tell you a little bit about*

our organization and our aim. [Insert information about your organization's history, values, and services here."

(This is to address the client's worries and explain your company's history and goal; this will help them know more about your brand.)

Agent: *"As a small, independently-owned firm, we are able to provide a degree of personalized care and attention to detail that may not be available with a bigger, nationally-branded organization. We are sincerely devoted to our community and to assisting our customers in reaching their real estate objectives."*

This is to underline the importance of partnering with a locally owned and operated business.)

Agent: *"In addition to the advantages of working with our organization, I feel that my experience and competence as an individual agent make me the greatest alternative for you. [Details about your skills, experience, and client-facing approach matters here."*

(This is to precisely discuss the benefits of working with you; this includes you adding your skills, experience, and how you have been able to close in clients in your past experience as a realtor.)

Agent: *"If you wanted to talk with former clients who have worked with our organization and me, I would be pleased to give references or testimonials,"* says the agent. *I feel that hearing directly from clients who have worked with an agent is the greatest approach to appreciate the value of their services."*

(This is to offer references or testimonials from previous clients. This will help you to back up what you have said you are good at.)

Agent: *"I recognize you have a choice when it comes to choosing an agent, and I would be thrilled to have the opportunity to earn your business," says the agent. My experience, skill, and devotion to my clients make me the greatest choice for you, in my opinion. I hope you will allow me to show it to you."*

(Like any other script, this is to request the opportunity to gain their business and look forward to signing up a contract with them)

It is not about how big a firm is that makes a transaction successful; it is about the commitment and experience of the realtor.

9. I MUST FIRST CONSULT WITH MY HUSBAND.

The 'I need to talk to my husband' objection usually arises for two reasons. First, it appears that a person perceives probable pain in investing in your product or service compared to the value they would obtain from the investment.

People buy for two reasons: to escape suffering and to achieve pleasure or a desired goal.

If a person believes that they will not achieve their desired outcome for the investment they will have to make, they may use the I need to talk to my spouse argument to avoid purchasing.

The second reason the "I need to talk to my spouse" excuse happens is that the cost of having the product or service may not be affordable for them. In addition, family conflicts may arise if things are not correctly done, which is typically the more reasonable explanation for this sales issue.

So now you know why the client will want to do this, how will you tackle this objection?

This script just made it easy:

Agent: *"I entirely understand the value of making decisions as a group, and I respect your want to talk things over with your husband. Selling a house is a huge financial and emotional choice, and it's critical that everyone be on the same page."*

(This emphasizes the necessity of making decisions as a group.)

Agent: *"If you'd like, I'd be pleased to set up a time to talk about this more with both you and your husband. We can go through the current market circumstances, your home's characteristics, and your goals and priorities in further depth, and I can answer any questions you may have."*

(This is to schedule a time to discuss this more with the client.)

Agent: *"As a real estate agent, I have a thorough grasp of the local market as well as the needs of buyers and sellers, and I can utilize this expertise to assist you in making educated decisions about how to price and advertise your house. In addition to my professional experience, I am dedicated to providing great customer service and collaborating closely with my customers to meet their requirements and goals."*

(This is to underline the importance of your knowledge and resources.)

Agent: *"I recognize that you have options when it comes to choosing an agent, and I would be happy to gain your business. My experience,* *skill, and devotion to my clients make me the greatest choice for you, in my opinion. I hope you will give me the opportunity to show it to you."*

(This is to request the opportunity to gain their business.)

The summary of this solution is for you to have an extensive discussion with both the prospect and her husband, which solves it. Let the husband be abreast of new updates.

10. WE ARE WILLING TO WAIT BEFORE PURCHASING A HOUSE.

This usually happens when the buyer is not ready to commit and is unsure when they will be able to enter the market. As a result, the script should focus on pinpointing and addressing their issues to increase the buyer's trust and improve their willingness to purchase the house. Here is how :

Agent: *"I realize that you have opted to postpone your home purchase, and I respect your decision. It's natural to want to thoroughly analyze your alternatives and ensure that you're making the greatest decision for your family and future. However, bear in mind that the real estate market is continuously changing, and understanding current market circumstances and how they may affect the availability and cost of properties in your target location can be beneficial."*

(This is to accept the client's decision to wait and emphasize the necessity of considering current market circumstances.)

Agent: *"I feel that now is an ideal time to buy based on my study of the local market and your unique requirements and preferences. The location, condition, and qualities of the property, as well as the broader market circumstances, can all have an impact on the availability and pricing of houses. While it is true that market circumstances can change over time, it is also crucial to remember that there are numerous variables that can impact the availability and pricing of properties, making it impossible to anticipate when the market will be most beneficial for purchasers."*

(This is to give a market study and explain the aspects that might impact housing availability and pricing.)

Agent: *"While it may be tempting to put off buying a property, it is vital to remember that there are hazards to doing so. The longer you wait, for example, the more competition you may encounter from other buyers, which might impact the availability and cost of properties in your selected location. Furthermore, if you rent while you wait, you may continue to pay out large sums of money without accumulating any equity or ownership in a home."*

(This is to highlight the possible hazards of waiting to buy.)

Agent: *"If you're unsure whether you should purchase now or wait, I'd be pleased to supply you with further information and tools to assist you in making an informed decision. This might contain a market study, current market circumstances, trends, or advice from other industry specialists. My primary goal is to assist you in achieving* *your real estate objectives and obtaining the best possible outcome for your property purchase".*

(This offer provides additional information and resources to assist you in making an educated decision.)

11. BEFORE PURCHASING THE HOME, I WOULD LIKE TO LIST AT LEAST 100 ISSUES DURING THE INSPECTION.

You understand that your client wants to request everything on the inspection report. Still, you also have to let them know that traditionally you would instead focus on items that are physically broken or have a health and safety issue rather than wasting time on all items on the list. However, you must be careful not to sound like you are hiding something from them. So this is how you nail that:

Agent: *"I can respect your want to be thorough and address any potential problems with the property, so I understand why you want to put a lot of stuff on the inspection objection."*

(This is to acknowledge the client's request to list numerous issues on the inspection objection; we are doing this.)

Agent: *"The inspection objection is a crucial step in the negotiation process because it enables you to discover any problems or difficulties with the property and ask the seller to fix or otherwise address them before closing. It's crucial to remember that the inspection objection is not meant to be a comprehensive list of all potential problems with the property, but rather a list of significant issues that could negatively impact the house's usefulness or worth."*

(The goal of the inspection objection and how it could impact the negotiation process are explained here.)

Agent: *"I would recommend a more reasonable amount of items, such as [insert number] items or less, given the aim of the inspection objection. This will enable you to concentrate on the crucial problems and conduct a fair and reasonable negotiation with the vendor."*

(This is to add a few more practical issues to the inspection objection list and ensure to proceed with the contract. If not immediately, always tie it to a date.)

12. I DON'T BELIEVE WE SHOULD ACCEPT THE DEAL AS IS.

Suppose this objection is raised; in that case, you must show that you understand entirely. Remind them that the only thing you will do today is submit an offer and put an option on the home to decide later whether you still want to leave it or move forward.

This script will make doing that easier for you:

Agent: *"I entirely appreciate it if you're unsure whether you want to submit an offer for the property. It's totally reasonable to have reservations and worries because purchasing a home is a significant decision. I'm here to assist you in navigating the procedure and to give you the knowledge and direction you need to make a wise choice."*

(This is to acknowledge the client's skepticism and assure them that having reservations before making a significant purchase is typical.)

Agent: *"Could you elaborate on your worries or reservations? Is there a particular issue that has you on edge? I can provide you with the information and assistance you need to proceed with confidence if I am aware of your worries."*

(This is to ensure the client is prompted to express doubts or worries.)

Agent: *"I would be pleased to give you further details or resources if you need them to make an informed choice. This could contain a market analysis, details on the state and developments of the market, or suggestions from other business experts. I want to make sure you are aware of all your alternatives and that you choose wisely based on your requirements and objectives."*

(The goal is to help the client make an informed decision by offering to provide more resources and information.)

Agent: *"While it's crucial to carefully weigh your options and make sure your choice is the right one for you, it's equally crucial to remember that making an offer could come with both risks and rewards. For instance, if you put off making an offer too long, you can miss out on a home that fits both your wants and your budget. On the other hand, you might not be able to negotiate a favorable bargain if your initial offer is too low or unrealistic. I can assist you in weighing the advantages and disadvantages of making an offer so that you can decide what is best for you."*

(This is to underline both the possible rewards and hazards of making an offer; this is done.)

13. I WILL PURCHASE THE PROPERTY DIRECTLY FROM THE LISTING AGENT BECAUSE I DON'T WANT TO USE A BUYER'S AGENT.

This objection always arises when the client thinks they will save on commission by going directly to the listing agent. But what they do not know is that the issue is the listing agent has their client's best interest in mind, not yours. You now explain to them why they will need someone with their best interest in mind to ensure you get the best deal possible.

You can do that perfectly with this script:

Agent: *"I can see your desire to streamline the process and I realize that you want to buy directly from the listing agent. However, it's vital to remember that a buyer's agent can offer a variety of beneficial advantages that can aid you in achieving your real estate objectives."*

(This is to appreciate the client's wish to work directly with the listing agent while outlining the advantages of using a buyer's agent.)

Agent: *"Also a buyer's agent is a real estate expert who only works for you and represents the buyer's interests. A buyer's agent can assist you in finding homes that fit your needs and budget, negotiating the best price and terms, and navigating the challenging home-buying process. A buyer's agent can also enable you to avoid any hazards or errors by offering insightful information on the neighborhood market, the property, and the seller."*

(This is to justify the need to clarify the function of a buyer's agent and how the customer might benefit from one.)

33

Agent: *"I have the skills and resources you need as a knowledgeable and committed buyer's agent to help you realize your real estate objectives. I am dedicated to giving my customers the finest service and representation possible since I have a thorough awareness of the local market and the needs of buyers and sellers. I firmly feel that my knowledge and commitment make me the greatest person to assist you in achieving your real estate objectives."*

(This is done to underline the need to hire a knowledgeable, committed buyer's agent.)

Agent: *"I am aware that you have a choice in agents, and I would consider it an honor to have the chance to win your business. I sincerely hope that you will give me the opportunity to show you the advantages of dealing with a buyer's agent. Together, let's look for the ideal house for you and your family."*

(I'm doing this to request the chance to win their business.)

14. I'M WORRIED ABOUT MY LEASE SINCE I DON'T WANT TO BREAK IT.

Usually, when your client is concerned about breaking their lease, they always bring it up as an objection. But they do not know that you can help them negotiate the right deal that will cover the cost of breaking their lease rather than them popping money into someone else's pocket.

You can execute that with this script:

Agent: *"You're worried that you might breach your lease, and I entirely understand that. Many buyers have this common worry, so it's crucial to carefully weigh all of your options before making a choice."*

(This is to let the client know that we understand their anxiety about breaking their lease and let them know that it is a frequent worry for many buyers.)

Agent: *"I can provide you details regarding the procedure for breaking a lease and any possible repercussions, if you'd like. This can contain details regarding any fines or charges you might have to pay as well as any legal or contractual responsibilities you might have. You can make an informed choice about whether to break your lease by being aware of these facts."*

(This is a request for information on breaking a lease and any associated penalties.)

Agent: *"Depending on your specific situation, there can be other ways to manage your lease that can help you reach your real estate objectives without violating it. You might be able to sublet the house or transfer the lease to someone else, for instance. I can provide you additional details about these possibilities and assist you in finding the best course of action."*

(Offer substitute suggestions for handling the lease.)

Agent: *"I have years of experience working with clients in comparable circumstances, so I have a thorough understanding of the neighborhood market and the requirements of buyers and sellers. I can provide you* *the knowledge and tools you need to get through the procedure and decide what is best for your circumstances. Let's collaborate to create a solution that satisfies your requirements and enables you to accomplish your real estate objectives."*

(This is done to underline how beneficial it is to work with a real estate agent with experience.)

15. I DON'T BELIEVE WE SHOULD ACCEPT THE DEAL AS IS.

Firstly, Suppose this kind of objection is raised. In that case, you have to show that you understand entirely and that the only thing you will do today is submitting an offer and put an option on the home to decide later whether you still want to leave it or move forward.

This script will make doing that easier for you:

Agent: *"I entirely appreciate it if you're unsure whether you want to submit an offer for the property. It's totally reasonable to have reservations and worries because purchasing a home is a significant decision. I'm here to assist you in navigating the procedure and to give you the knowledge and direction you need to make a wise choice."*

(This is to acknowledge the client's skepticism and assure them that having reservations before making a significant purchase is typical.)

Agent: *"Could you elaborate on your worries or reservations? Is there a particular issue that has you on edge? I can provide you with the information and assistance you need to proceed with confidence if I am aware of your worries."*

(This ensures the client is prompted to express doubts or worries.)

Agent: *"I would be pleased to give you further details or resources if you need them to make an informed choice. This could contain a market analysis, details on the state and developments of the market, or suggestions from other business experts. I want to make sure you are aware of all your alternatives and that you choose wisely based on your requirements and objectives."*

(The goal is to help the client make an informed decision by offering to provide more resources and information.)

Agent: *"While it's crucial to carefully weigh your options and make sure your choice is the right one for you, it's equally crucial to remember that making an offer could come with both risks and rewards. For instance, if you put off making an offer too long, you can miss out on a home that fits both your wants and your budget. On the other hand, you might not be able to negotiate a favorable bargain if your initial offer is too low or unrealistic. I can assist you in weighing the advantages and disadvantages of making an offer so that you can decide what is best for you."*

(This is to underline both the possible rewards and hazards of making an offer; this is done.)

16. I WILL PURCHASE THE PROPERTY DIRECTLY FROM THE LISTING AGENT BECAUSE I DON'T WANT TO USE A BUYER'S AGENT.

This objection always arises when the client thinks they will save on commission by going directly to the listing agent. But what they don't know is that the listing agent has *their* client's best interest in mind, not yours. You can now explain why they need someone working with their best interest at heart to ensure they get the best deal possible.

You can do that perfectly with this script:

Agent: *"I can see your desire to streamline the process and I realize that you want to buy directly from the listing agent. However, it's vital to remember that a buyer's agent can offer a variety of beneficial advantages that can aid you in achieving your real estate objectives."*

(This is to appreciate the client's wish to work directly with the listing agent while outlining the advantages of using a buyer's agent.)

Agent: *"Also a buyer's agent is a real estate expert who only works for you and represents the buyer's interests. A buyer's agent can assist you in finding homes that fit your needs and budget, negotiating the best price and terms, and navigating the challenging home-buying process. A buyer's agent can also enable you to avoid any hazards or errors by offering insightful information on the neighborhood market, the property, and the seller."*

(This is to justify the need to clarify the function of a buyer's agent and how the customer might benefit from one.)

Agent: *"I have the skills and resources you need as a knowledgeable and committed buyer's agent to help you realize your real estate objectives. I am dedicated to giving my customers the finest service and representation possible since I have a thorough awareness of the local market and the needs of buyers and sellers. I firmly feel that my knowledge and commitment make me the greatest person to assist you in achieving your real estate objectives."*

(This is done to underline the need to hire a knowledgeable, committed buyer's agent.)

Agent: *"I am aware that you have a choice in agents, and I would consider it an honor to have the chance to win your business. I sincerely hope that you will give me the opportunity to show you the advantages of dealing with a buyer's agent. Together, let's look for the ideal house for you and your family."*

(I'm doing this to request the chance to win their business.)

17. I'M WORRIED ABOUT MY LEASE SINCE I DON'T WANT TO BREAK IT.

Usually, when your client is worried about breaking their lease, they always bring it up as an objection. But they do not know that you can help them negotiate the right deal that will cover the cost of breaking their lease rather than them popping money into someone else's pocket.

You can execute that with this script:

Agent: *"You're worried that you might breach your lease, and I entirely understand that. Many buyers have this common worry, so it's crucial to carefully weigh all of your options before making a choice."*

(This is to let the client know that we understand their anxiety about breaking their lease and let them know that it is a frequent worry for many buyers.)

Agent: *"I can provide you details regarding the procedure for breaking a lease and any possible repercussions, if you'd like. This can contain details regarding any fines or charges you might have to pay as well as any legal or contractual responsibilities you might have. You can make an informed choice about whether to break your lease by being aware of these facts."*

(This is a request for information on breaking a lease and any associated penalties.)

Agent: *"Depending on your specific situation, there can be other ways to manage your lease that can help you reach your real estate objectives without violating it. You might be able to sublet the house or transfer the lease to someone else, for instance. I can provide you additional details about these possibilities and assist you in finding the best course of action."*

(Offer substitute suggestions for handling the lease.)

Agent: *"I have years of experience working with clients in comparable circumstances, so I have a thorough understanding of the neighborhood market and the requirements of buyers and sellers. I can provide you* *the knowledge and tools you need to get through the procedure and decide what is best for your circumstances. Let's collaborate to create a solution that satisfies your requirements and enables you to accomplish your real estate objectives."*

(This is done to underline how beneficial it is to work with a real estate agent with experience.)

18. I DON'T SEE HOW YOUR OFFER CAN HELP ME.

Most realtors see this as an objection, but if well scrutinized, one would realize it is more of an opportunity than an objection. The potential client doesn't know what your offer entails and wants to see if it can immensely benefit him.

Realtors see this as a setback when a potential buyer comes up with this and gets discouraged. Be confident and use open-ended questions to make him understand how your property will be the best for them.

Here is a script that could be of help:

Agent: *"Thanks for being honest, and I agree with you. What exactly do you desire to have in a home?"*

Client: responds

Agent: *"I can see that you are a lover of good things, and you won't believe this property has all you mentioned. It even has this and that which might be of additional benefit to you."*

(Let them understand that the home has all the qualities they desire and even more and explain everything in detail.)

Agent: *"Do you see these needs you mentioned as urgent or a future plan?"*

Client: (selects)

Agent: *"Why do you see it as (that option)?"*

(Help your client gradually see why your offer might be vital to them. Let them unveil the reasons by themselves. Clients are better convinced this way.)

Agent: *"Now you have realized why my offer can be of help. I appreciate your time and patience. You can consider it further and reply with your final decision."*

19. I AM MUCH MORE PLEASED WITH YOUR COMPETITOR.

This is one of the saddest objections most realtors find challenging, but you do not need to be emotionally distressed; you are unique and do not need to see everyone as a competitor. The client might not even have any contract with another competitor, and most clients say this when they are uninterested.

Agent: *"I agree with you. Competitor X is a great firm; I have heard excellent things about them. Every real estate firm is unique; my firm's uniqueness is why we have achieved this and that."*

(Do not tarnish the image of your competitor, as it makes your client think you are jealous. Instead, let your client realize that your firm is unique and list your achievements.)

Agent: *"I am pleased you have a contract with Competitor X. Is there any information you would like to know, or do you have any questions about the property?"*

(This is where you will know whether the client has a contract. If there is a contract on the ground, the conversation will be smooth, while some clients might come clean to you at this point that they are just not interested.)

Agent: *"These are the ways our company can help you solve these questions. We have also bought similar properties for our clients, which were successful without any hitch. Would you like to have our contact in case you will need our help in the future?"*

(This is to let them know you have the solution they want.)

You just hit the nail on the head! Your potential client is probably attracted to you, and you might have a new client in the future or at the moment.

20. THIS ISN'T MY PRIORITY AT THIS MOMENT.

Most realtors would probably say something like 'I understand' without understanding why the client came up with such an objection. Most clients that come up with this objection are just confused and nothing else. They do not have a clarification of the questions on their mind yet, and they sum it up that they are not interested in it at the moment.

This is a script that helps the client correctly determine if it is a priority or not.

Agent: *"Hey, lovely potential client. I would like to know your priorities now if you are comfortable telling me and see how my firm can make your preferences a reality."*

(Agree with your prospect. Try to know their priorities.)

Agent: *"Oh, I see! Those are lovely priorities. Can you tell me those things unique in the things you have mentioned that make them top on your list?"*

Client: (list them)

Agent: *"I am conversing with you to ask if you will be interested in checking out some properties that suit your priorities perfectly. I will send pictures to you, and we can go and check them out together if you are interested".*

(This is to convince the client that you have other properties that might be unique to their desire.)

This script helps you turn a lemon into lemonade by discovering what is on your prospect's mind.

21. JUST SEND ME THE DETAILS OF THE HOUSE.

This objection is usually raised when the realtor has not been able to properly educate the prospect on how the home would be suitable for the prospect. The prospect is confused and gets tired of the conversation. This script will help you, as a realtor, handle this objection better.

Agent: *"To confirm. Are you, Mr. so and so, interested in property X?"*

(Chances are that you are speaking to the wrong person, and you might need to check your lead qualification to ensure that the person is qualified to get the property.)

Client: *"Yes."*

Agent: *"I understand you are still confused about the information I gave you as regards the property. I am ready to help you clear your doubts."*

(All you are trying to do here is to assure the prospect that you are patient enough for them to understand.)

Client: *"I have no doubts whatsoever."*

Agent: *"Can you tell me what you love about this property?"*

(Some clients are still unconvinced and might want to brush you off by telling you they have no doubts. This response will help you discern if they are not just interested or if they genuinely do not understand.)

Agent: *"I will like to explain again, if you do not mind."*

(Explain until your prospect understands and ask questions if they are still interested.)

22. HOW DID YOU KNOW THAT I AM INTERESTED IN PURCHASING A PROPERTY?

Most realtors see this as aggressive, but it is an opportunity to let the prospect know how to find a good client for a property.

Here is a sample script

Agent: *"Hi, Mr. Lovren. I am glad you asked that question. A realtor employs several legal ways to find the perfect client for their dream property. Social media platforms like Facebook, Twitter, and LinkedIn can be of help as they easily connect prospects that need their dream property with our platforms. We could also get the information from the customer request section on our website."*

(List the ways you employ to get a client for a property and let the prospect understand that you are not tracking him illegally.)

23. I DON'T WANT TO GAMBLE WITH MY MONEY AGAIN.

This objection usually comes up when a prospect has experienced disappointment in the past and needs a realtor they can trust.

To erase the prospect's doubt, you must show them your past achievements and let them understand that you have sold properties similar to the one they are currently interested in. Carefully explain how you handled the transaction and how everything went smoothly with evidence.

Finally, you might connect them with your clients, and their testimonies will convince them of your credibility.

Agent: *"Sir, I have been practicing for several years, and I have successfully handled several transactions similar to yours. If you do not mind, I would like us to fix a date when I can show you evidence of previous successful transactions that I have done. I will happily connect you with the clients I purchased similar properties for."*

24. I AM SORRY, BUT I DO NOT WANT TO PURCHASE ANYMORE. I WILL GET BACK TO YOU AT A BETTER TIME.

The prospect might raise this objection either because they are unhappy with the transaction process or not convinced anymore. All you need to do is to revise your transaction process first to check out what you are doing wrongly. Call his attention and apologize to them if you can figure out one. If you can't find any, ask them if they would like some improvement in the services rendered to them.

Here is a script that can be of help

Agent: *"Hi. We revised our transaction process and discovered that we were doing something wrong. We are sorry for that, and it will be rectified as soon as possible."*

(If nothing was found)

Agent: *"Hi. We understand you do not want a purchase for now, and we stand with you. Is there anything you would like us to improve on?"*

Client: Yes(he mentions it)

Agent: *"We will work on that, sir, and we appreciate that you noticed that error. We also apologize for any inconvenience it might have cost you. You can now be assured that we will give you the best services after correcting the lapses you discussed. We will still like you to transact with us."*

(The way to any prospect's heart is to show that you care about their concern.)

25. THE PROPERTY IS LOCATED IN A FLOOD ZONE.

Buyers may be concerned about purchasing a property in a flood zone, particularly if they have experienced flooding or live in an area prone to natural disasters. This is the script you can use to implement that:

Agent: *"I understand that purchasing a property located in a flood zone can be a concern, particularly if you have experienced flooding in the past. However, it's essential to remember that flood zone properties may have lower property values and can be a more affordable option."*

(The aim of this is to communicate to them that you comprehend and empathize with the difficulties they are encountering and to inspire them to recognize the favorable aspects of their present circumstance.)

Agent: *"We can work with the seller to obtain more information about the specific risks and precautions that can be taken to mitigate flood damage, such as flood insurance or building elevations."*

(The purpose of this is to acknowledge and honor their decisions and exhibit a solid dedication to meeting their requirements.)

26. THE PROPERTY IS LOCATED IN A BUSY OR CONGESTED AREA.

Buyers may have concerns about living in a busy or congested area, mainly if they prefer a quieter and more peaceful environment.

Agent: *"I understand that living in a busy or congested area may not be ideal for everyone, and finding a property that aligns with your lifestyle preferences is essential."*

(The intention behind this is to convey to them that you understand and sympathize with their challenges and motivate them to acknowledge the positive aspects of their current situation.)

Agent: *"However, properties located in busy areas can offer convenience and accessibility to amenities such as shopping, dining, and public transportation. We can explore other neighborhoods that may better fit your needs if you prefer a quieter environment."*

(This aims to value and esteem their choices while deeply committing to fulfilling their needs.)

27. THE PROPERTY HAS A COMPLICATED LEGAL HISTORY.

Buyers may have concerns about purchasing a property with a complicated legal history, mainly if they are concerned about potential legal issues or liabilities.

Agent: *"I understand that the legal history of a property can be a concern for buyers, particularly if you are worried about potential legal issues or liabilities. However, we can work with legal professionals to review the property's legal history thoroughly and identify potential problems or risks."*

(The purpose is to indicate to them that you value and understand the struggles they're going through and to motivate them to recognize the beneficial components of their present state.)

Agent: *"We can also work with the seller to obtain more information and negotiate any necessary legal agreements or resolutions."*

(The aim is to show acknowledgment and honor for their decisions while also exhibiting a strong dedication to meeting their requirements.)

28. THE PROPERTY NEEDS TO BE CLOSER TO AMENITIES AND SERVICES.

Buyers may be concerned about purchasing a property that is too far from amenities and services, particularly if they value convenience and accessibility.

Agent: *"I understand that having access to amenities and services is an essential consideration for buyers, particularly if you value convenience and accessibility. However, remember that living in a more remote location can offer unique advantages, such as more privacy and quiet."*

(The goal is to communicate to them that you comprehend and identify with the difficulties they're experiencing and encourage them to acknowledge the advantageous aspects of their current situation.)

Agent: *"We can work with you to identify properties that are within a reasonable distance to the amenities and services you need or explore options for bringing these services closer to your property."*

(The intention behind this is to appreciate and value their choices and to showcase a sincere determination to satisfy their needs.)

29. THE PROPERTY IS LOCATED IN A FLOOD ZONE.

Buyers may have concerns about purchasing a property located in a flood zone, particularly if they have experienced flooding in the past or live in an area prone to natural disasters. This is the script you can use to implement that:

Agent: *"I understand that purchasing a property located in a flood zone can be a concern, particularly if you have experienced flooding in the past. However, it's important to remember that flood zone properties may have lower property values and can be a more affordable option."*

(The aim is to communicate to them that you comprehend and empathize with their difficulties and inspire them to recognize the favorable aspects of their present circumstance.)

Agent: *"We can work with the seller to obtain more information about the specific risks and precautions that can be taken to mitigate flood damage, such as flood insurance or building elevations."*

(This aims to acknowledge and honor their decisions and strongly commit to meeting their requirements without fail.)

30. THE PROPERTY IS TOO LARGE.

Buyers may have concerns about purchasing a too-large property, particularly if they do not need the additional space or are concerned about maintenance and upkeep costs.

Agent: *"I understand that having too much space can be a concern for buyers, particularly if you are concerned about maintenance and upkeep costs. However, keep in mind that a larger property can offer unique advantages, such as more room for entertaining and hosting guests."*

(The aim is to demonstrate to them that you understand and sympathize with the obstacles they're confronting and to motivate them to recognize the beneficial elements of their current condition.)

Agent: *"We can work with you to identify more manageable-sized properties or explore options for maximizing the space within a larger property."*

(This aims to recognize and esteem their decisions while also showing a profound dedication to meeting their requirements.)

31. THE PROPERTY IS TOO SMALL.

Buyers may have concerns about purchasing a too-small property, particularly if they have a growing family or need more space.

Agent: *"I understand that having enough space is an important consideration for buyers, particularly if you have a growing family or need room for other activities."*

(This is meant to let them know that you grasp and empathize with their difficulties and motivate them to see the bright side of their present circumstance.)

Agent: *"However, keep in mind that a smaller property can offer unique advantages, such as lower maintenance costs and more* *intimate living space. We can work with you to identify properties with more space or explore options for maximizing the space within a smaller property."*

(This aims to acknowledge and respect their choices while demonstrating a strong commitment to fulfilling their needs.)

32. THE PROPERTY IS LOCATED IN A HIGH-CRIME AREA.

Buyers may be concerned about purchasing a property in a high-crime area, particularly if they value safety and security.

Agent:: *"I understand that the safety and security of a property are important factors in your decision-making process. However, keep in mind that crime rates can fluctuate over time, and it's important to conduct thorough research and due diligence on the area before making a purchase."*

(The objective here is to show them that you appreciate and relate to their challenges and inspire them to acknowledge the positive aspects of their current state.)

Agent: *"We can work with you to obtain information about crime rates in the area and explore options for additional security measures, such as home security systems or neighborhood watch programs."*

(This aims to show recognition and admiration for their decisions while also exhibiting a deep commitment to meeting their requirements.)

33. THE PROPERTY IS PRICED TOO HIGH.

Buyers may have concerns about purchasing a property that is priced too high, particularly if they are on a tight budget or looking for a good deal.

Agent: *"I understand that the price of a property is a crucial factor in your decision-making process, and it's important to find a property that is within your budget."*

(This is designed to demonstrate to them that you understand and share their obstacles and to motivate them to recognize the benefits of their present situation.)

Agent: *"However, keep in mind that the asking price of a property may be negotiable, and we can work with the seller to obtain a fair and reasonable price based on market conditions and comparable properties. Additionally, we can explore other properties that may be more affordable and better suited to your needs and preferences."*

(The intention behind this is to appreciate and regard their choices and to showcase a genuine determination to satisfy their needs.)

34. THE PROPERTY HAS A HISTORY OF PREVIOUS OWNERS.

Buyers may have concerns about purchasing a property with a history of previous owners, particularly if they need clarification on the condition or maintenance of the property.

Agent: *"I understand that the history of previous owners can be a concern for buyers, particularly if you need clarification on the* *condition or maintenance of the property. However, keep in mind that a history of previous owners can also mean that the property has been well-maintained and cared for over the years."*

(The intention behind this is to make them feel heard and understood in their struggles and to encourage them to focus on the advantages of their current state.)

Agent: *"We can work with the seller to obtain more information about the history of ownership and maintenance and conduct a thorough inspection of the property to ensure that it is in good condition before you make a purchase."*

(This aims to recognize and honor their decisions while also showing a profound commitment to meeting their requirements.)

35. THE PROPERTY HAS A UNIQUE LAYOUT OR DESIGN.

Buyers may be concerned about purchasing a property with a unique layout or design, particularly if they need the best help utilizing the space.

Agent: *"I understand that the layout or design of a property can be a concern for buyers, particularly if it is not what you are accustomed to. However, keep in mind that a unique layout or design can offer creative opportunities for customization and personalization."*

(The aim of this is to convey to them that you comprehend and sympathize with the difficulties they are encountering and to inspire them to see the positive elements of their current situation.)

Agent: *"We can work with interior designers or home renovation professionals to help you envision how the space can be utilized and customized to fit your needs and preferences."*

(The goal is to acknowledge and esteem their choices while demonstrating a strong devotion to fulfilling their needs.)

36. THE PROPERTY IS LOCATED IN A REMOTE OR ISOLATED AREA.

Buyers may have concerns about living in a remote or isolated area, mainly if they prefer a more urban or suburban lifestyle.

Agent: *"I understand that living in a remote or isolated area may not be ideal for everyone, and finding a property that aligns with your lifestyle preferences is essential. However, properties located in remote areas can offer privacy, peace, and quiet and may be more affordable."*

(This is designed to let them know that you comprehend and share their struggles and to encourage them to see the bright side of their current state.)

Agent: *"We can explore other neighborhoods that may better fit your needs if you prefer a more urban or suburban environment."*

(This aims to respect and recognize their decisions while showing a solid devotion to meeting their requirements.)

37. THE PROPERTY NEEDS TO BE BIGGER FOR THE BUYER'S NEEDS.

Buyers may have concerns about purchasing a property that is either too small or too big for their needs, particularly if they are looking for a long-term residence.

Agent: *"I understand that the size of a property is an important factor in your decision-making process, and it's important to find a property that meets your specific needs."*

(The objective here is to make them feel understood and supported in their difficulties and to encourage them to see the advantages of their present situation.)

Agent: *"However, keep in mind that properties that are either too small or too big can be customized to fit your lifestyle with minor modifications such as furniture or renovations. If this property doesn't meet your size requirements, we can explore other properties that may better fit your needs."*

(The intention behind this is to appreciate and acknowledge their choices and to demonstrate a profound commitment to fulfilling their needs.)

38. THE PROPERTY HAS TOO MANY REPAIRS OR RENOVATIONS NEEDED.

Buyers may have concerns about purchasing a property that requires extensive repairs or renovations, particularly if they need to prepare to invest the necessary time and money to make the property livable.

Agent: *"I understand that the condition of a property is a crucial factor in your decision-making process, and it's important to find a property that meets your standards. However, keep in mind that properties that require repairs or renovations may be more affordable and offer the potential for a higher return on investment."*

(This aims to demonstrate to them that you appreciate and relate to the obstacles they are experiencing and inspire them to recognize the beneficial aspects of their current state.)

Agent: *"We can work with contractors or home improvement professionals to obtain estimates for repairs or renovations and factor these costs into your budget. Additionally, we can explore other properties that may require fewer repairs or renovations if this concerns you."*

(This aims to recognize and value their decisions while showcasing a sincere dedication to satisfying their needs.)

39. THE PROPERTY HAS A HISTORY OF PEST INFESTATIONS.

Buyers may be concerned about purchasing a property with a history of pest infestations, particularly if they need to prepare to deal with the potential health and safety hazards.

Agent: *"I understand that the presence of pests can be a major concern for buyers, and it's important to find a property that is free of pests. However, keep in mind that pest infestations can be mitigated with professional pest control services and preventative measures."*

(This is meant to communicate to them that you grasp and empathize with their challenges and motivate them to acknowledge the favorable aspects of their present circumstance.)

Agent: *"We can work with the seller to obtain more information about the history of pest infestations and take appropriate measures to ensure that the property is free of pests before you move in."*

(The objective is to show appreciation and respect for their choices while also exhibiting a deep commitment to meeting their requirements.)

SELLERS OBJECTIONS

40. WHY SHOULD WE PICK YOU?

This is a very common question most curious clients ask. They have probably worked with inferior agents and have the impression that you are similar. Some of these clients might be considering FSBO(For Sale by Owners). They feel the extra commission you will be paid is burdensome, which is normal, especially for novice sellers.

This is when your current knowledge comes into play. Help them understand that recent studies have shown that FSBOs fetch much less than agent-monitored properties.

Most sellers also need to realize they will pay a commission if the buyer uses an agent. They have nothing to lose by using a realtor; you must let them know that. They also do not thoroughly understand documentation and purchase agreements as much as a realtor does. This lack of knowledge can lead to serious problems either presently or in the future.

Besides, realtors know how to market a house. They also know what to look for in a house, making it a good quality house. They can tell if a house will last for several years or if it is just a fluke. Realtors study this in higher institutions, so they have the knowledge and experience to handle the sale and purchase of houses better than anybody else. These are the things you tell your client(s) to convince your client that they need a realtor.

Moreover, show your past successful transactions and achievements. Assure them that you are bound not to disclose any private information that will not implicate you. They gain confidence in you and become comfortable hiring you. This script will help you tailor your conversation to convince the potential client.

Agent: *"I recognize that selecting the appropriate agent is a huge choice, and I appreciate you taking the time to consider me. I am convinced I can offer you the required care and experience."*

(To acknowledge the significance of their choice and thank them for even considering you in the first place, and for them to raise that type of question as an objection, they see the possibility of you and them working together, you just have to play your cards well.)

Agent: *"I have X years of real estate expertise and a proven track record of assisting my customers in buying and selling houses in the region. I'm also an XYZ real estate association member, taking additional X and Y training. These abilities and experiences have provided me with a thorough awareness of the local market and how to manage the real estate transaction."*

(This is where you will sell yourself to the client by describing your experiences and life achievements. You can call it a show-off, but this is where you will pitch yourself to the customer by declaring your experiences and life achievements.)

Agent: *"I take pleasure in being a devoted and attentive agent that constantly prioritizes the requirements of my customers. I'm accessible to answer your questions and give direction throughout the process, and I'll do all in my power to make your experience as pleasant and stress-free as possible."*

(To demonstrate your commitment to your clientele and to reassure them that they are in excellent hands.)

Agent: *"Based on my expertise and commitment to my customers, I feel I am the greatest choice to assist you in buying or selling your house. May I get the opportunity to work with you and demonstrate my worth?"*

(This is to solicit their business; their response will tell you whether they are interested in working with you.)

Remember to emphasize your unique selling points and how you can bring value to the client's experience. It's also crucial to project confidence without seeming arrogant and to demonstrate that you're prepared to go above and beyond to satisfy their demands.

41. DO YOU ALREADY HAVE A BUYER?

This is yet another typical real estate seller complaint. The customer does not want to employ you, does not want to meet with you, and does not want to hear your sales pitch about how linking sellers and buyers is what you do for a livelihood and how you can do it for them.

They only want to chat if you can bring a customer with you on the first day. This is a difficult objection, and it's difficult because you have to educate them on how the process works and understand their present goal without making them incorrect or feel stupid.

Here's a script for doing it perfectly:

Agent: *"I appreciate you inquiring about my customers. It's a prevalent problem among vendors, and I'm delighted to address it."*

(This is to acknowledge their inquiry and thank them for their interest in the buyers.)

Agent: *"As a real estate agent, I am responsible for advertising your house to potential purchasers and selling it for the highest feasible price. To reach purchasers, I employ a variety of marketing tactics, including putting your home on the MLS (multiple listing service) and other web platforms. Use social media and other internet methods to promote your property, Organize open houses and private showings for prospective buyers, and network with other agents and industry experts to discover possible purchasers."*

(This is to discuss your marketing approach. You may alter this to suit your best marketing strategy while also ensuring you are not boring them with unrelated and pointless information. Also, keep it brief and straight to the point.)

Agent: *"I am committed to finding a buyer for your house and will work tirelessly to sell it for the highest potential price. I have a proven* *track record of selling properties and am confident I can bring your home in front of the correct purchasers."*

(To stress your dedication to finding a buyer. This will let them understand that you are working hard to assure their satisfaction.)

Agent: *"I feel I'm the ideal candidate to assist you in selling your house based on my marketing approach and track record of successful sales. May I get the opportunity to work with you and demonstrate my worth?"*

(This is more like a call to action to ask for their business. This sentence does this without appearing aggressive.)

When answering this issue, keep your marketing plan and track record of successful sales in mind. Underlining your dedication to finding a buyer and selling the home for the highest feasible price is critical.

42. HAVE YOU SOLD ANY HOMES IN MY NEIGHBORHOOD?

This is a straightforward objection to solve; all you need is preparation. It would help if you were adequately prepared for this objection, as it is also very common. Ensure that all the details of the past properties you have sold are properly kept in a storage file.

You can even take it further to create your own website or a social media platform where all the necessary information is displayed. After assuring the clients that you have experience selling homes in their neighborhood, simply direct them to the website/platform where they can see everything you have said.

Here is the script that knocks this objection out.

Agent: *"I appreciate you inquiring about my expertise in your field. It's a frequent problem both buyers and sellers share, and I'm pleased to address it."*

(This is to acknowledge their inquiry and thank them for enquiring about the number of houses you have sold in their neighborhood.)

Agent: *"I've sold a lot of properties in your neighborhood and have a thorough grasp of the local market. For example, I just sold a home in the XYZ area with a layout and price range identical to yours. The seller got many bids and sold the house for more than the asking amount. I also have a lot of satisfied clientele in the region who would gladly assist me."*

(This is to offer relevant instances of your experience in their field, and this line illustrates how knowledgeable you are in their field.)

Agent: *"Besides having sold properties in the region, I have a thorough awareness of the local market. I remain current on trends and statistics and can offer significant insights and recommendations on what to expect in the present market. This knowledge and skills, I feel, will be useful to you as we work together to buy or sell your house."*

(To underline your understanding of the local market, which will allow you to explain why your experience and skills with the local market would benefit them if they hire you.)

Agent: *"I feel I am the ideal candidate to assist you in purchasing or selling a house based on my expertise and understanding of the local* *market. May I get the opportunity to work with you and demonstrate my worth?"*

(This is to ask for their contract with you; like any other script, there must be a call to action at the end of your script.)

Remember to emphasize your relevant experience and expertise in the local market when responding to this point. Demonstrating that you have a track record of accomplishment in the field and can give the customer significant insights and guidance is critical.

43. I'M NOT PLANNING TO DO ANYTHING; IT'S FINE AS IS.

Despite being urged to solve several issues, the seller says the house is good and does not require any improvements. So all you have to do here is to explain to the seller how making some updates is the standard and applies to many homes. And also it influences the sales of the home positively.

So if you encounter this kind of objection, all you have to do is to use this script to clarify your points:

Agent: *"I understand your desire to sell the property as-is, and I appreciate the opportunity to represent you. I wish you the best of luck with the sale."*

(This is to recognize their choice and thank them for notifying you of their intentions about the property.)

Agent: *"Can you tell me why you decided to sell the home as-is? I'm always searching for ways to grow and learn, and your opinion might be quite beneficial."*

(This is to ask for more information; this is how you find out why they have decided to leave it as is for sale. The clients will give various reasons ranging from financial to personal, which will lead to a whole new discussion, but in any case, the following script should help you draw a valid)

Agent: *"Even though we will not be collaborating on this transaction, I would like to be a resource for you in the future. Don't hesitate to get in touch with me if you have any questions or need assistance with real estate in the region. I'm always willing to assist."*

(This is to position oneself as a valuable resource for clients in the near future; it shows how concerned you are and that you are excited to work with them soon.)

Agent: *"I wish you the best of success with the sale of your house and hope everything goes as planned. Thank you for taking the time to consider me, and I hope to hear from you again in the future."*

(This ensures you conclude the talk positively and on good terms with them.)

Remember to be cordial and professional even if the customer decides not to work with you. You never know when you might get to work with them again or when they might suggest friends or family to you.

44. ACCORDING TO ZILLOW, OUR HOUSE IS WORTH THIS.

We've all heard that you can't rely on a Zestimate. But, whether we like it or not, Zillow is the most frequently utilized real estate portal globally, so prospects are likely to believe it.

Remember, even though you're going toe-to-toe with Zillow in this scenario, you shouldn't frame the platform as your competitor. Instead, position yourself as a Zillow partner, someone who assists people in making the most of the platform.

Once you have a prospect's trust, you can begin to educate them on why a Zestimate is not the most accurate assessment of their property and why you are a better choice.

Agent: *"I saw that Zestimate! That's something I wanted to elaborate on. After all, we listed 30 houses on Zillow last year, and it's a fantastic platform. But I wanted to let you know that the initial Zestimate on all 30 homes was at least 15% off. In one case, by 40%."*

(This is to let them know that you know the Zestimate and are familiar with Zillow. Also, to let them know how the estimate can be off from the actual value.)

Agent: *"Why? Because there are no Zillow agents in the area to evaluate your home! Zillow attempts to compute a market average using an algorithm. However, your buyers will not care about a Zestimate because at the end of the day, it's their idea of the value of the home that makes the price."*

(This is to inform them about how Zillow comes up with their estimate and why it is not usually accurate with the property's true value.)

Agent: *"If a Zestimate is 15% lower, you will lose 15% on the sale. If it's 15% higher, no one will buy the house, and you'll lose money on negotiating. Wouldn't you rather sell your house for the highest possible price and get the most money?"*

(This is to tell them about the Zestimate's consequences.)

45. WE ARE SURE OUR HOME IS UNIQUE; THE RIGHT BUYER HASN'T COME THROUGH YET.

Every home offered by a seller is usually considered unique to them, and it is understandable because they haven't seen as many homes as you. But what they probably should not believe is being unique makes their house stand out and this will help it sell. You have to let them know that if they are willing to get the right buyer, they must be willing to put in the effort to market it.

Here is a script that you could use to handle this objection:

Agent: *"I understand that you believe your home is unique and that the right buyer just hasn't come through yet. It can be frustrating to wait for the perfect buyer to come along, especially if you feel that your home is special and deserves a higher price."*

(This is to acknowledge the seller's perspective.)

Agent: *"However, it is important to remember that marketing your home effectively is crucial to finding the right buyer. As a professional real estate agent, I have the skills and experience necessary to effectively market your home and reach a wider pool of potential buyers. I can use various marketing techniques, including online advertising, targeted outreach, and open houses, to generate interest in your home and find the right buyer."*

(This is to emphasize the importance of marketing.)

Agent: *"For example, I can create a personalized marketing plan for your home that highlights its unique features and targets potential* *buyers who are interested in homes like yours. I can also provide tips and guidance on preparing your home for sale and making it more appealing to potential buyers. And, if any issues or complications arise during the sale process, I can help you navigate them and find a solution."*

(This is to offer specific examples of how you can help.)

Agent: *"I would love the opportunity to work with you and help you sell your unique home. Can we schedule a time to meet and discuss the next steps in more detail?"*

(This is to ask for the opportunity to work with them.)

Agent: *"Thank you for considering me as your real estate agent. I look forward to the opportunity to work with you and help you achieve your real estate goals."*

(This is to thank them for considering your services.)

46. IF WE LOWER THE PRICE, WE WON'T HAVE ENOUGH EQUITY TO MOVE TO OUR NEW HOME.

What if your seller won't drop the price despite being on the market a while? Let the seller know it's typical to drop the price at least once or twice, especially when the home is dwindling on the market.

Here is a script that you could use to handle this objection:

Agent: *"I understand that you are concerned about lowering the price of your home and not having enough equity to move. It can be difficult* *to decide to lower the price, especially if it means you will not have as much money to put towards your next home."*

(This is to acknowledge the seller's concerns.)

Agent: *"However, it is important to remember that pricing your home correctly from the start is crucial to getting it sold. A properly priced home will generate more buyers' interest and ultimately lead to a higher sale price. If your home is priced too high, it may sit on the market for a longer period of time and ultimately sell for less than it would have if it were priced correctly from the start."*

(This is to emphasize the importance of pricing)

Agent: *"It may also be helpful to consider the current market conditions and the state of the local real estate market. If the market is competitive and there are many buyers interested in homes like yours, it may be possible to negotiate a higher price. On the other hand, if the market is slow and there are not many buyers, it may be more difficult to negotiate a higher price."*

(This is to discuss the current market conditions.)

Agent: *"If you would like, I can provide you with a market analysis to give you a better understanding of the current state of the market and help you determine the right price for your home. This will allow you to make an informed decision about whether to lower the price or hold out for a higher offer."*

(This is to offer a market analysis)

Agent: *"Regardless of what you decide, I am here to support you and offer my professional guidance. Please don't hesitate to reach out to me if you have any questions or need any assistance. I am always here to help."*

(This is to respect their decision and offer to stay in touch.)

47. I WANT TO WAIT FOR A MORE REASONABLE OFFER BECAUSE THIS OFFER IS LOW.

Objections like this arise when sellers have a strong will that the house should value more than it was offered. But Ask them Questions like this, "Are you willing to roll the dice for a 1% chance?" and "How long will it take before you get another offer?". This will help open a better discussion phase that will help them make better decisions faster.

Here is a script that you could use to handle this objection:

Agent: *"I understand that you feel the offer is too low and that you want to wait for a more reasonable offer. It can be frustrating to receive an offer that does not reflect the value of your home."*

(This is to acknowledge the seller's concerns.)

Agent: *"However, it is important to remember that the first offer is often just a starting point for negotiations. As your real estate agent, I can help you negotiate a better price for your home by presenting counter-arguments and highlighting the unique features and value of your property."*

(This is to emphasize the importance of negotiating.)

Agent: *"It may also be helpful to consider the current market conditions and the state of the local real estate market. If the market is competitive and there are many buyers interested in homes like yours, it may be possible to negotiate a higher price. On the other hand, if the market is slow and there are not many buyers, it may be more difficult to negotiate a higher price."*

(This is to discuss the current market conditions.)

Agent: *"If you would like, I can provide you with a market analysis to give you a better understanding of the current state of the market and help you make an informed decision about whether to accept the offer or hold out for a higher price."*

(This is to provide a market analysis.)

Agent: *"Regardless of what you decide, I am here to support you and offer my professional guidance. Please don't hesitate to reach out to me if you have any questions or need any assistance. I am always here to help."*

(This is to respect their decision and offer to stay in touch.)

48. I'VE ALREADY HAD MANY INTERESTED BUYERS COME THROUGH MY HOUSE, AND I BELIEVE I'LL BE ABLE TO SELL IT IN A WEEK. SO, WHY SHOULD I HIRE YOU?

You can't change the fact that they don't want to sell. However, keep exploring to see whether they have an underlying motive to sell now. Can you overcome their reluctance to sell? But, and I mean BUT, you might be able to get inside their heads and figure out what makes them so hesitant to sell. Also, explain to them how the frequent visitation of the buyers without any returning actions from them does raise the chance of getting it sold faster.

Here's a script you could use to handle this objection:

Agent: *"I'm glad to hear you're getting a lot of interest in your house and believe you'll be able to sell it within a week. That is a fantastic achievement and demonstrates that you did an excellent job of marketing your home and attracting potential buyers."*

(To emphasize the importance of professional representation.)

Agent: *"While you may be able to sell your house on your own, employing a real estate agent has a number of advantages. As a professional agent, I have the knowledge and experience to negotiate the best price for your home, protect your interests, and handle all of the paperwork and details that come with the sale."*

(To acknowledge the objection as well as the seller's success.)

Agent: *"For example, I can assist you in determining the appropriate price for your home by conducting a market analysis and educating you on current market conditions. I can also handle all of the paperwork and make sure that everything is done correctly and on time. And, if any problems or complications arise during the sale process, I can assist you in resolving them."*

(To provide specific examples of how you can assist.)

Agent: *"I would be honored to work with you and assist you in selling your home for the highest possible price. Can we arrange a time to meet and go over the next steps in greater detail?"*

(This is to request the opportunity to work with them.)

Agent: *"Thank you for taking the time to consider me as your real estate agent. I am excited about the chance to work with you and assist you in achieving your real estate objectives."*

(This is to express gratitude for their consideration of your services.)

49. WE WANT TO WAIT FOR THE MARKET TO RECOVER BEFORE SELLING IT AGAIN.

Can you get around their unwillingness to sell? Definitely No! But, and I mean BUT, you might want to keep digging to see if they have an underlying motivation. Then you remind them of that and why they decide to sell in the first place.

Here's a script you could use to handle this objection:

Agent: *"I understand your desire to wait for the market to recover before attempting to sell your home again. It can be frustrating to try to sell a home when the market is not in your favor."*

(This is done to acknowledge the objection and to comprehend their reasoning.)

Agent: *"However, the real estate market is constantly changing, and waiting for the market to recover may take longer than you expect. By selling now, you can move on to your next home or investment while potentially taking advantage of current market conditions. Being proactive and considering all of your options is always a good idea."*

(This is to emphasize the advantages of selling now.)

Agent: *"If you are concerned about market conditions, I would be happy to conduct a market analysis to help you understand the current state of the market. This will enable us to devise a strategy to maximize the value of your home and sell it for the highest possible price."*

(This is to examine the current market situation and present it to them)

Agent: *"If you decide to proceed with the sale, I will be there to help you every step of the way. I can give you advice and tips on how to prepare your home for sale and effectively market it to attract potential buyers."*

(This is an offer to assist them in preparing for a sale.)

Agent: *"Thank you for taking the time to consider me as your real estate agent. I am excited about the chance to work with you and assist you in achieving your real estate objectives."*

(This is to thank them for considering your services.)

50. WE ARE OPEN TO LISTING AFTER THE HOLIDAYS.

Most sellers are still holding on to their homes and hiding behind the umbrella of holidays. Still, as a realtor, you must let them know that a certain percentage of the properties advertised for sale actually sell. So it will be crucial for them to get a head start on their competitors in the real estate market.

Here's a script you could use to handle this objection:

Agent: *"I understand why you want to list your home after the holidays. The holidays can be a hectic and stressful time, and it's understandable that you'd prefer to focus on something else right now."*

(This is to acknowledge the objection and comprehend their reasoning.)

Agent: *"The real estate market, on the other hand, is continuously changing, and there may be possibilities to sell your house sooner than you think. You might be able to take advantage of current market circumstances and sell your property for top price if you list now. It's always a good idea to be proactive and plan for the possibility of a sale."*

(This is to emphasize the advantages of listing now.)

Agent: *"If you'd like, I'd be pleased to give you some pointers and advice on how to prepare your property for sale so that when you're ready to market, you'll be in the greatest position to obtain the best price for it. Is there anything in particular you require assistance with?"*

(This is to let them know that you are willing to give them more information and details about their property sales.)

Agent: *"I understand if you prefer to wait until after the holidays. Please do not hesitate to contact me if you have any questions or require any assistance in the meantime. I am always available to assist."*

(To respect their decision and offer to stay in touch.)

Agent: *"Thank you for taking the time to consider me as your real estate agent. I hope to have the opportunity to work with you in the future."*

(This is to express gratitude for their consideration of your services.)

51. IF WE HAVE ALREADY INFORMED YOU THAT WE WILL NOT BE LISTING OUR HOME UNTIL NEXT YEAR AND THAT WE WILL CONTACT YOU WHEN WE ARE READY, WHY ARE YOU STILL CALLING US?

If you write a follow-up letter that prospects find helpful, you can call them the following month and discuss what you wrote. But if you send the same old real estate stuff that everyone else sends and on and on, you'll just come across as a pest.

Here's a script you may use to avoid being seen as a threat.

Agent: *"I apologize if my calls were bothersome. I understand you have decided to postpone listing your home until next year, and I respect your decision."*

(To acknowledge the objection and express regret for any inconvenience.)

Agent: *"However, I wanted to remind you that the real estate market is always changing and that there may be opportunities to sell your home sooner than you anticipated. You may be able to take advantage of current market conditions and sell your home for top* *dollar if you list now. Being proactive and preparing for the possibility of a sale is always a good idea."*

(To emphasize the advantages of listing now.)

Agent: *"If you'd like, I'd be happy to give you some pointers and advice on how to prepare your home for sale so that when you're ready to list, you'll be in the best position to get the best price for it. Is there anything in particular you need assistance with?"*

(This is an offer to assist them in preparing for a future listing.)

Agent: *"I understand if you prefer to wait until next year. Please contact me if you have any queries or require any support in the meanwhile. I am always willing to assist."*

(To show respect for their decision and to offer to stay in touch.)

Agent: *"Thank you for taking the time to consider me as your real estate agent. I hope to have the opportunity to work with you again in the future."*

(This is to express gratitude for considering your services)

52. WE HAVE DECIDED ONLY TO WORK WITH AGENTS WHO HAVE GIVEN US CLIENTS WHILE WE WERE SELLING ON OUR OWN.

Agents are classified into two categories. There are listing agents and buying agents. Of course, both listing and selling, but let them consider this, among the two types, which one do they believe will result in the sale of their home? An agent who sells one person at a time or an agent who sells to the masses? This will hasten their decision-making.

Certainly! Here's a script you could use to deal with this objection:

Agent: *"I understand your desire to work with an agent who has referred clients to you while you were selling on your own. That demonstrates that they are proactive and willing to go above and beyond to find buyers for your property."*

(To acknowledge the objection and the feelings underlying it.)

Agent: *"As an experienced real estate agent, I have a proven track record of marketing and selling properties similar to yours. I am well-versed in the local market and understand how to effectively target potential buyers."*

(To highlight your abilities and experience.)

Agent: *"In the last year, for example, I have sold numerous residences in the same price range and neighborhood as yours. To create interest and secure a sale, I employed a number of marketing strategies, including internet advertising, open houses, and targeted approach to possible purchasers."*

(To provide concrete instances of your previous successes.)

Agent: *"Please let me know if you have any specific concerns about my ability to sell your property. I am confident in my ability to address them and provide you with the support and guidance you require to achieve your real estate objectives."*

(To address any particular concerns they may have)

Agent: *"I would be delighted to work with you and assist you in selling your property. Can we set up a time to meet and go over the next steps in greater detail?"*

(To request the opportunity to work with them.)

53. ACCORDING TO ONE OF THE EXPIRED POSTINGS, THE PREVIOUS REALTOR NEVER VIEWED OUR HOUSE, NOR DID ANYBODY ELSE FROM HIS BUSINESS.

This objection is to build their trust in you and explain to them how your office's agents are not too busy to make them a priority. And that you pledge to promote their house to agents who sell properties rather than agents who do not.

Here is a script that you might use to deal with the objection.

Agent: *"I understand your concerns, and I sincerely apologize if you had a bad experience with the previous agent who listed your home. As a real estate agent, it is my purpose to give the finest quality of service to my customers and to do all possible to assist them reach their real estate objectives."*

(To address the client's concerns and apologize for any poor experiences they may have had with past agents.)

Agent: *"I approach showings personally and believe that the listing agent should be present for showings whenever possible. This allows me to answer any potential buyers' questions and highlight the unique features of your property. I will also take a variety of efforts to promote your home to the maximum number of possible purchasers,* *including holding open houses, promoting the property online and through traditional marketing methods, and utilizing my broad network of real estate industry connections."*

(This conveys the importance of your approach to showings and your efforts to highlight the property.)

Agent: *"I would be pleased to share further information about my approach to showings and marketing, or if you have any special concerns or queries. I can also look into various solutions or tactics that might help you reach your goals while keeping your budget and other limits in mind. Let's collaborate to develop a solution that matches your demands while also assisting you in achieving your real estate goals."*

(This is an opportunity to share more information about your approach and explore potential solutions.)

54. WHY SHOULD WE PICK YOU ABOVE ALL THE OTHER REALTORS WE'VE SPOKEN WITH?

The only way to answer this question is to understand what distinguishes you from other agents. Because each agent is distinct... That one is entirely up to you. Also, make sure you explain how your marketing strategies are different from other agents...

Here's a script you could use to make doing that easy;

Agent: *"I understand your inquiry, and I appreciate the opportunity to explain why I believe I am the best candidate to represent your interests in the sale of your property. I have a deep understanding of* *the needs of buyers and sellers as a real estate professional with many years of experience in the local market, and I use that knowledge to develop marketing techniques that are tailored to my clients' needs and goals."*

(To acknowledge the client's question and explain the importance of your experience and expertise.)

Agent: *"My approach to promoting and selling real estate comprises a variety of activities aimed to reach out to potential buyers and highlight the distinctive aspects of my clients' properties. This encompasses both classic marketing means like print and direct mail, as well as internet marketing via websites, social media, and other platforms. I also use my substantial real estate industry network to assist advertise my customers' properties to potential purchasers."*

(To describe your strategy for promoting and selling real estate.)

Agent: *"In addition to my experience and expertise, I am committed to providing excellent customer service and keeping open and frequent conversation with my clients throughout the selling process. I understand that selling a home can be a stressful and emotional experience, and I strive to make the process as easy and stress-free for my clients as possible."*

(This is to justify the importance of your customer service and communication abilities.)

Agent: *"I would be pleased to share additional information about my approach to promoting and selling properties, as well as answer any specific issues or questions you may have. I can also supply references* *from happy customers who can attest to the high quality of my work. Let's collaborate to develop a solution that matches your demands while also assisting you in achieving your real estate goals."*

(This is to give references and further information about your procedure.)

55. WE'D WANT TO CONSIDER IT BEFORE SELLING.

This objection shows how indecisive the sellers can be about a decision they have already concluded on but are still in between selling or not—explaining the effects of both actions to them. Hence, they know how critical it can be to delay action. This should end with a call to action line to make them commit to their decision.

Here's a script you may use to deal with the argument

Agent: *"I realize that you need some time to consider things through, and I accept your decision totally. Making a choice to sell your home is an important and often emotional process, and it is critical that you take the time necessary to make the best decision for you and your family."*

(To demonstrate your awareness of the client's need to take some time to study their alternatives.)

Agent: *"Please let me know if there is any other information or resources I can give to assist you make an informed decision. I am here to guide you through the process of selling your home in a way that matches your requirements and expectations."*

(To give extra information or resources that may benefit the decision-making process.)

Agent: *"Would you mind if I followed up with you in a few days to see if you have any additional questions or if there is anything else I can do to help you make your decision? I want to make certain that you have access to all of the information and resources you require to make the greatest option for you and your family."*

(To request permission to contact the client at a later time.)

Agent: *"Thank you for considering me for your real estate needs. I am excited about the chance to work with you and assist you in achieving your real estate objectives."*

(To express gratitude to the client for their time and concern.)

56.WE WANT TO COMPARE WHAT YOU SAY TO WHAT OTHER REALTORS SAY.

Whenever this objection comes up, it is either they don't have a good understanding of your marketing plan for their house, or they believe the agent can give them a better offer, but all you have to do is to explain fully how your marketing techniques are distinct and what will make your service stand out amidst other agents. And finally, ask them what exactly is keeping them from picking up the pen and signing their home with you.

Here is a script that you might use to deal with the objection.

Agent: *"I understand that you want to compare the information I'm providing to that of other real estate agents, and I respect your desire to consider all of your options before making a decision. As a real* *estate expert, I have a thorough awareness of the local market and the needs of buyers and sellers, and I apply that knowledge to create a marketing plan targeted to your specific needs and goals."*

(To recognize the client's desire to compare your information to that of other real estate agents and to convey the benefit of your method.)

Agent: *"My approach to promoting your home comprises a variety of activities geared to reach out to potential buyers and highlight the unique attributes of your property. This encompasses both classic marketing means like print and direct mail, as well as internet marketing via websites, social media, and other platforms. I also use my substantial real estate business network to assist advertise your home to potential purchasers."*

(The purpose of this section is to describe your approach to promoting the property.)

Agent: *"While comparing the information provided by different real estate agents can be beneficial, it is critical to carefully evaluate all of the factors that can affect the value of your property in order to obtain the best possible outcome. Different agents may take different approaches to marketing and pricing, and it is critical to carefully evaluate each of these approaches to determine which one is best suited to your needs and goals."*

(This is to discuss the possible disadvantages of comparing information from several real estate agents.)

Agent: *"I would be pleased to offer you with further information about my approach to promoting your home, or if you have any special issues or queries. I can also look into various solutions or tactics that might help you reach your goals while keeping your budget and other limits in mind. Let's collaborate to develop a solution that matches your demands while also assisting you in achieving your real estate goals."*

(This is an opportunity to share more information about your approach and explore potential solutions.)

57. WE WANT TO LIST HIGH AND THEN LOWER THE PRICE LATER.

This is a good strategy only if the market is rising and it will sell like hotcakes. However, when the market is ranging, which happens most of the time, it is an inferior strategy. Try to explain this to your client and let your client understand this concept in simple terms. The seller needs essential expertise and education on the current real estate market. Show your client the current market prices and advise them to sell competitively.

Here is the script:

Agent: *"I realize you want to market your home at a high price and then lower it later if required. This is a method that some sellers employ, and it may be effective in a rising market. This strategy, however, has certain risks and downsides. For example, if your house is much more expensive than comparable homes in your neighborhood, it may be less appealing to buyers and take longer to sell."*

(To acknowledge the client's approach and discuss the potential risks and disadvantages of wanting to penetrate the market with the high price before reducing it later on.)

Agent: *"Based on my understanding of the local market and the data I have obtained on comparable homes, I would propose pricing your house at a competitive price from the outset. This can help you attract more buyers and boost the likelihood of a successful sale. If you'd like, I can give you more facts and data to back up my advice."*

(The goal here is to give statistics and market insights to back up your proposal and what you have termed to be risks to them.)

Agent: *"If you are still interested in starting at a higher price and then adjusting the price later, we may explore different pricing tactics that may be more effective. For example, we may begin with a higher asking price and then add a price adjustment option in the listing agreement that permits us to lower the price if necessary at a later date. This gives us the freedom to make changes while still presenting your house competitively in the market."*

(Now, this is a crucial part of not leaving them hanging; here, you will propose alternate pricing solutions that will work perfectly for their house.)

Agent: *"Finally, remember that one of the most crucial components in a successful sale is accurately valuing your house from the outset. If you overprice your house, you risk losing potential buyers and extending the sales process. Pricing your house appropriately from* *the outset, on the other hand, can help you attract more buyers, negotiate a better sale price, and sell your home faster."*

(This line underscores the necessity of accurately valuing the house from the outset.)

They will appreciate it if you help them realize that they would have been exposed to many risks if they had not informed you.

58. YOU ARE OVERBURDENED WITH LISTINGS, AND WE WANT SOMEONE TO GIVE US THE ATTENTION WE DESERVE.

The key to this objection management script is to focus on the past triumphs that have carried you ahead. If you have 50 properties for sale, you have a track record that speaks for itself.

These are the same outcomes they will want for their deal. If someone has a few properties, they are unlikely to have the same amount of experience. So let them know that when it comes to obtaining the most for their home in today's market, efficiency is not something they should chastise someone for.

So how do you do this without having to lose them? Is this script the key to that?

Agent: *"I realize you want an agent who will offer you the attention and assistance you need during the house-selling process. I can guarantee you that, despite the fact that I now have a lot of listings, I am devoted to giving customized service to each and every one of my clients. I focus on my client's requirements and make time to answer any questions or concerns they may have."*

(This is to address the client's worries and reassure them of your availability, even when you have a lot of listings with you.)

Agent: *"As a busy real estate agent, it is critical for me to keep organized and manage my workload properly in order to give my customers the best service possible. I utilize a range of tools and processes to remain on top of my schedule and give my clients the attention they need. I would be pleased to answer any particular concerns you may have regarding how I would manage my workload while working with you."*

(Here, you will have to explain how you intend to manage your workload and keep organized in this section; also, ensure you let them know that no client is more important than the other, so they have nothing to worry about.)

Agent: *"I would be pleased to give references or testimonials if you would want to talk with some of my prior clients to get a sense of the quality of care and attention I deliver. I feel that hearing directly from my clients is the greatest way to comprehend the level of care and attention I deliver."*

(This is too to give references or testimonials from prior clients about how great you have been able to manage multiple homes.)

Agent: *"I recognize that you have options when it comes to choosing an agent, and I would be happy to gain your business. My experience, skill, and devotion to my clients make me the greatest choice for you, in my opinion. I hope you will give me the opportunity to show it to you."*

(To request the opportunity to gain their trust with their home and strike up a deal already!)

Ensure that they understand that it is an organization that matters irrespective of the workload and that you have the efficient tools to do that.

59. I'VE SEEN THIS MARKETING STRATEGY USED BY OTHER AGENTS; WHAT DISTINGUISHES YOURS?

There are only so many things an agent can do to sell a house, and the final choice is determined by how you feel about the person representing you, not by what you do differently.

So, tell me, what attributes do you want in an agent?

Here's a script you may use to respond to this objection:

Agent: *"I understand you've seen comparable marketing strategies from other agencies and are asking what sets mine apart. While there are certain basic aspects to good real estate marketing, I think that tailoring a plan to the particular requirements and goals of each individual client is the key to success. I take the time to get to know my clients and their homes, and I utilize that information to design a tailored marketing campaign that will successfully highlight their home's unique characteristics and benefits."*

(This addresses the client's problems while emphasizing the unique parts of your marketing strategy and what makes it stand out.)

Agent: *"Some of the particular methods and approaches that I may employ to advertise your home are as follows:*

- *Creating high-quality marketing materials, such as professional photography and a comprehensive property brochure*

- *Making use of internet platforms and social media to reach a larger audience*

- *Organizing open houses and other activities to attract potential buyers*

- *Finding possible purchasers via networking with other brokers and industry professionals.*

- *Negotiating with buyers and other brokers to get the best deal for my customers."*

(Here, this is to explain the precise methods and approaches you will employ to advertise their property)

Agent: *"In addition to my customized marketing approach, I feel my experience and track record of success set me apart as an agent. I've been in the real estate industry for a long time and have a thorough awareness of the local market as well as the demands of buyers and sellers. I have a demonstrated track record of effectively promoting and selling homes for my clients, and I think that my knowledge and ability will help you sell your house."*

(This is to highlight your achievement experience and track record with your marketing strategies.)

Agent: *"I recognize that you have options when it comes to choosing an agent, and I would be happy to gain your business. I believe that my unique approach to marketing, combined with my experience and track record of success, make me the best choice for you. I hope you will give me the opportunity to show it to you."*

(As usual, this is to request the opportunity to call them to strike a deal, having cleared their objections)

Your achievements will defend you in the case of this objection.

60. WHY IS YOUR PROPOSED LISTING PRICE CONSIDERABLY LOWER THAN THE OTHER BROKERS?

Your seller feels that you underpriced their house and that another realtor could obtain a higher price. All you need to do is to engage the seller in determining what they feel the house is worth and clarify your aim – to sell the home fast and for the highest amount of money possible based on current market data.

Here's a script you may use to do that without a hiccup;

Agent: *"I realize you are worried about the disparity in suggested listing prices supplied by different agents. It's natural to have concerns and want to ensure you're making an educated decision. I want to reassure you that my major priority is to assist you in achieving your real estate objectives and obtaining the greatest possible price for the sale of your house."*

(This is mainly to address the client's worries and reassure them that you are looking out for their best interests, including getting them the value for their money.)

Agent: *"To calculate the proposed listing price for your house, I did a thorough research of the local real estate market and took several criteria into account, including, comparable properties in your neighborhood that have previously sold or are presently on the market, Your house's features and condition, and the demand for real estate in your region.*

Based on this data, my proposed listing price is competitive and represents current market circumstances. It is also crucial to note that the buyer and seller's discussions set the final sale price of a house and that the listing price is only a starting point for those talks."

(This is where the work is; this is where you will have to explain to justify your pricing approach and the variables you evaluated in this section.)

Agent: *"I would be pleased to supply extra information or statistics to back my proposed listing price, I can also give you a comprehensive study of comparable houses in your region."*

(This is to explain how you will be ready to give them further information about your suggestion and provide additional facts or evidence to support your recommendation.)

Agent: *"Ultimately, it's crucial to remember that pricing your house appropriately from the outset is one of the most critical components in a successful sale. If you overprice your house, you risk losing potential buyers and extending the sales process. Pricing your house appropriately from the outset, on the other hand, can help you attract more buyers, negotiate a better sale price, and sell your home faster. When is a good time to come by?"*

(This underscores the necessity of accurately valuing the house from the outset rather than rushing through the process.)

And finally, like usual, always ensure that you call them to action at the very end of each script like this one; this is to ensure that the effort you have put into conversing with them is not in vain and is rewarded by them striking up a contract with you.

61. WE'RE NOT QUITE READY YET; WE'D WANT TO RENOVATE THE HOUSE BEFORE PUTTING IT ON THE MARKET.

You can typically understand why individuals don't think they're ready to purchase or sell, as you can with most "not on the market" concerns.

For example, if you discover that they believe they may buy the house for a higher price, demonstrate how you can deliver tremendous value before the selling process begins. This way, no one needs to feel obligated to do anything for which they are not truly prepared.

Here is a script that you can use to deal with the objection.

Agent: *"I realize you want to make a few renovations to your property before listing it for sale. Making renovations and repairs to a house may frequently raise its value and make it more desirable to purchasers. However, you must be smart about which projects you take on since some will have a higher influence on the sale price than others. If you'd like, I can provide some recommendations for prioritizing your initiatives based on their potential effect as well as the time and money they'll take."*

(This is to appreciate the client's desire to enhance their house and provide ideas for project prioritization to show that you are with them on that motion.)

Agent: *"While it might be tempting to wait until your house is totally ready to market, it's vital to bear in mind that there are also benefits to listing sooner rather than later. For example, the real estate market is ever-changing, and waiting too long to list your house may result in missing out on good market circumstances."*

(The more time and money you spend on maintenance, repairs, and staging, the longer your house remains on the market. Buyers are more likely to make an offer on a property currently on the market than on a home that has not yet been listed)

Describe the advantages of listing sooner rather than later.

(This is to help stage the house, provide repairs and improvements recommendations, and also ensure you describe the advantages of listing sooner rather than later.)

Agent: *"If you are not yet ready to list your house, I can still assist you make it ready for the market. I may give ideas for presenting the home to make it more appealing to purchasers, as well as assist you in prioritizing any necessary repairs or renovations. We can get your house in the greatest possible condition for a successful sale if we work together."*

(This is to guide them through the next step since you have already informed them why it is better to list sooner rather than later.)

Agent: *"I recognize you have a choice when it comes to choosing an agent, and I would be thrilled to have the opportunity to earn your business. My experience, skill, and devotion to my clients make me the greatest choice for you, in my opinion. I hope you will give me the opportunity to show it to you."*

(This is finally to request the opportunity to gain their business and make them strike up a contract with you.)

62. I'D WANT TO LOCATE A HOME BEFORE PUTTING MINE ON THE MARKET.

You can overcome this objection to listing by stressing the process of purchasing or selling a house. You explain in it that whether buying or selling a house, you must consider the big picture - buying and then selling.

Here's a script you may use to address this objection like a realtor;

Agent: *"I realize you want to find a new house before placing your existing one on the market. It's natural to want to be sure you have somewhere to live before selling your present house, and I can surely assist you with both. As a real estate agent, I have access to a wealth of resources and tools that may assist you in finding your dream house and effectively selling your present one."*

(The primary reason here is to address the client's worries and reassure them that you can ideally assist with both jobs and save them the stress of finding someone to help them again.)

Agent: *"Selling and purchasing simultaneously might be a bit of a balancing act, but it can also have some significant advantages.*

For example, if you look for a new house before selling your old one, you may be more choosy and take your time finding the appropriate match.

Selling your present house first may give you greater negotiation power and flexibility when acquiring your new property.

You can avoid the need to relocate twice and the expenditures connected with temporary accommodation by selling and purchasing simultaneously.

You can also discuss items you can negotiate and ask for, such as a rent refund or a delayed settlement. Consider asking for a one-day listing; this strategy is attracting new prospects."

(This line explains the advantages of selling and purchasing simultaneously; it is more like an eye-opener for them.)

Finally, ensure you present yourself with some unique benefits of being both a Buyer and Seller agent for them and provide a call to strike a deal with you.

63. WE STILL HAVE ONE MORE AGENT TO INTERVIEW.

They don't see why they should pay you to sell the house, and that is not the real issue. The problem is that you haven't convinced them you can sell their house. You only need to show them your achievements and make them understand what you do differently from other agents.

Here is a script that you might use to deal with the objection and the lack of trust in your abilities;

Agent: *"I realize you are evaluating various agents and want to ensure you find the best fit for your requirements. Interviewing many agents is a wise idea since it allows you to evaluate various techniques and services and make an educated selection. Finding the proper agent, in my opinion, is critical to reaching your real estate goals and attaining the greatest possible outcome for the sale of your house."*

(This is to recognize the client's wish to interview numerous agents, telling them indirectly that you respect their decision and underline the significance of finding the ideal fit.)

Agent: *"I would be pleased to offer you with further information about my services and approach, I can also supply references or testimonials from former clients who can attest to the quality of care and attention I offer. I feel that hearing directly from clients who have worked with an agent is the greatest approach to appreciate the value of their services."*

(This is an invitation to share further information about your services and approach; using a client who has once been in their shoes as a testimonial will go a long way, but it is not compulsory; a normal client testimonial should do.)

Agent: *"In addition to my services and attitude, I feel that my expertise and track record of achievement set me apart as an agent. I've been in the real estate industry for a long time and have a thorough awareness of the local market as well as the demands of buyers and sellers. I have a demonstrated track record of effectively promoting and selling homes for my clients, and I think that my knowledge and ability will help you sell your house."*

(Continuing what you said earlier, you must highlight your experience and track record of achievement.)

Agent: *"I recognize that you have a choice when it comes to picking an agent, and I would be thrilled to have the opportunity to earn your business,"*

(This is mainly to let them know that even if they are finally going to go ahead with their decision, you are willing to help them along the way and are also open when they change their mind.)

Most clients would stick to their opinion, but the few you can convince will be loyal to you forever!

64. WE WANT TO SELL IT OURSELVES.

This typically indicates that a prospect does not understand how much work real estate brokers put in to sell a home.

They presumably read about the procedure online and concluded it wasn't too tricky. Perhaps they had a bad encounter with an agency in the past. In any case, attempt to gently uncover why they want to sell on their own and persuade them to realize how they can win more by working with you.

So this script is going to help you do that with ease:

Agent: *"I realize that you are interested in selling your house yourself, and I appreciate your desire to investigate all of your alternatives. However, I feel there are several advantages to dealing with a real estate agent, and I'd like to take the time to explain some of those advantages to you."*

(This is to acknowledge the client's wish to sell the house independently and convey the advantages of dealing with a real estate agent.)

Agent: *"As a real estate agent, I have access to a wide range of information and tools that can help you sell your house more successfully and for the greatest potential price. Some particular ways in which I may assist include: Offering a market study to assist you in determining the optimum listing price for your house, Using a number of media and platforms, marketing your house to a larger audience, Negotiating with purchasers and their representatives to get the best possible result for you, Getting through the legal and procedural components of the sale process."*

(This is to underline the importance of an agent's knowledge and resources for them to be aware of it and for that to also influence their decision.)

Agent: *"In addition to my knowledge and resources, I have a network of industry professionals and a track record of successful sales that can help you sell your house more quickly and effectively, For example, I might be able to introduce you to possible purchasers or link you to other specialists who can assist you with certain areas of the sale process."*

(This is to justify the importance of an agent's network and relationships and show them how it has influenced the successful sales of homes over the years.)

Agent: *"I recognize that you have a choice when it comes to picking an agent, and I would be pleased to have the opportunity to earn your business."*

(This is an invitation to gain their business and make them strike a contract with you.)

All they need is information and more information! Let them realize what they will lose if they proceed with this objection.

65. I'M JUST GOING TO SELL IT MYSELF.

Agents understand how to market a home using the best resources available. As a result, a seller who attempts to promote their home on their own will squander time and money on strategies that have not been proven to attract purchasers.

For instance, how might a seller enable an open house? Perhaps through signage placed across the area. While this may be efficient, they could not list the Open House on the MLS, shared by numerous websites such as Zillow.

Getting to the heart of the lead's motivation is a solid strategy to overcome this issue. Please do this by distinguishing between selling it and selling their house and determining which is essential to them.

You can implement the previous script as they serve the same purpose.

66. YOUR WORKPLACE IS NOT NEAR OUR HOUSE.

This excuse appears to be a smoke screen, and a smoke screen, I mean, this reason is just a camouflage. Clients often believe that your workplace has to be very close to the area where you have a listing and that, somehow, it will affect how you will help them with their property.

However, this script will help you debunk that without any hassle:

Agent: *"I appreciate you bringing up that you might have a problem about where our office is located, and I do understand why. Proximity is an important consideration in the real estate process because it allows us to be available to you and respond quickly to any needs or concerns that may arise."*

(Usually, this is to help you address the Client's concerns and emphasize the significance of proximity in the real estate process; nevertheless, you should be careful not to rule their opinion out badly but instead let your valid points speak for you.)

Agent: *"It is crucial to remember, however, that technology has enabled real estate agents to operate efficiently with customers regardless of their actual location. I have the capabilities and resources as a remote agent to give you the same level of care and attention as if I were in the same office. I am available to speak with you via phone, email, or video chat, and I can also use virtual tours and other resources to assist you in exploring properties and making educated selections."*

(This is to explain the advantages of working with a remote agent and expatriate well on how technology has helped realtors work more efficiently.)

Agent: *"I believe that, in addition to my ability to provide remote service, my experience and expertise as a real estate agent make me the best choice for you. [Insert details about your skills, experience, and client-facing approach here."*

(This emphasizes the importance of your experience and expertise with remote service.)

Agent: *"I would be happy to provide references or testimonials from previous clients who have worked with me if you would like to speak with them. I feel that hearing directly from clients who have worked with an agent is the greatest approach to appreciate the value of their services."*

(This is to give references or testimonials from prior clients.)

Agent: *"I understand that you have options when it comes to choosing an agent, and I would be honored to earn your business. My experience, skill, and devotion to my clients make me the greatest choice for you, in my opinion. I hope you will give me the opportunity to show it to you."*

(Finally, this is to request the opportunity to gain their business and strike a deal with them to continue the contract since the objection has been cleared.)

Technology is the key here, and it has made communication and research easier, which is the surest way to convince a client of this objection.

67. WE WILL LIST IT AFTER THE HOLIDAY.

Many homeowners and real estate brokers feel spring is the ideal season to sell real estate. After all, many individuals hibernate over the winter or are too preoccupied with the holidays to consider purchasing a new house. Buyers frequently begin their search in the spring to get established in their new homes before the start of the new school year.

However, the winter holiday season has advantages for house sellers as well. If you can't wait for the weather to warm up before putting your property on the market, you may take advantage of some of winter's unique benefits. Here is a script that you can use to deal with the objection:

Agent: *"I realize that you want to market your property after the holidays, and I appreciate your desire to look into all of your possibilities. However, bear in mind that the real estate market may be volatile, and there are frequent advantages to selling a house at a given period."*

(This is to respect the Client's desire to wait until after Christmas and to emphasize the advantages of listing now.)

Agent: *"Listing your property now, for example, may help us to capitalize on the busy holiday season, when there may be more buyers* *browsing for properties. Furthermore, advertising your house now may let us get a head start on marketing and attract more purchasers before the competition heats up in the spring."*

(This highlights the possible benefits of listing now rather than later.)

Agent: "On the other side, waiting until after the holidays to market your house may mean that you miss out on the opportunity to sell during the peak season, as well as having to compete with more listings in the spring. Furthermore, delaying listing may result in your house being on the market for a longer amount of time, which may be stressful and costly."

(This illustrates the potential disadvantages of waiting to list after the Holidays.)

Agent: *"If you're still undecided about when to list your house, I'd be pleased to do a market study and give recommendations based on current market circumstances and your unique objectives. My major purpose is to assist you in achieving your real estate objectives and obtaining the greatest possible price for the sale of your house."*

(The reason for this is to give market analyses and suggestions to your Client to show how willing you are to get them what they want in the market.)

Agent: *"I recognize that you have options when it comes to choosing an agent, and I would be happy to gain your business. My experience, skill, and devotion to my clients make me the greatest choice for you, in my opinion. I hope you will give me the opportunity to show it to you."*

(This is the final stage, where you request the opportunity to gain their business and strike a contract with them.)

Most people want to feel the holidays are usually quiet, which might also be a reason for this objection. However, most buyers browse for homes during this period as this might be their only spare time.

68. WE ARE ALREADY COMMITTED TO ANOTHER AGENT.

When other agents are mentioned, always check to see whether there's an arrangement in place. And an excellent way to go about this is to establish your argument and not be scared to compete a bit.

Here is a script that can assist you with that:

Agency: *"I understand that you are already committed to another agent, and I appreciate your decision to work with someone you feel comfortable with. It's vital to remember that selling a property is a huge financial and emotional choice, and finding the appropriate match in terms of both personal and professional compatibility is critical."*

(The main goal is to recognize the Client's commitment to another agency and to underline the significance of finding the proper fit.)

Agent: *"As a real estate agent, I am well-versed in the local market and the requirements of buyers and sellers. I have a demonstrated track record of effectively promoting and selling homes for my clients, and I think that my knowledge and ability can help you sell your house. In addition to my professional skills, I am also devoted to providing* *great customer service and to working closely with my customers to ensure their needs and goals are accomplished."*

(This is to discuss precisely the benefits of working with you and other unique benefits you will bring to the table if a contract is signed.)

Agent: *"If you would want further information about my services and approach, I would be pleased to supply it. I can also supply references or testimonials from former clients who can attest to the quality of care and attention I offer. I feel that hearing directly from clients who have worked with an agent is the greatest approach to appreciate the value of their services."*

(This is an invitation to share further information about your services and approach to the real estate market. It is more like pitching yourself.)

Agent: *"I recognize that you have options when it comes to choosing an agent, and I would be happy to gain your business. My experience, skill, and devotion to my clients make me the greatest choice for you, in my opinion. I hope you will give me the opportunity to show it to you."*

(The final call is to request the opportunity to strike a deal with them.)

This objection is usually false, and most prospects do that to scare you away at the first call. However, a little push is not bad, as they might realize you are not just another naive realtor.

69. HOW DO YOU SELL A HOUSE?

This usually comes up when the Client is willing to know more about how you sell homes and if you know your way around it. This objection is one of how clients often test if you are experienced and confident enough to be their realtor. Although this may seem unnecessary, you also want to carry your Client along every step in selling the house.

Here's a script you can use to perfectly answer that now that you know the intent of the Client:

Agent: *"Various actions must be completed to sell a house. Some of the specific tasks I perform as a real estate agent are as follows:*

Offering a market study to assist you in determining the optimum listing price for your house, Using several media and platforms, marketing your house to a large audience, Negotiating with purchasers and their representatives to get the best possible result for you, and Managing the legal and procedural requirements of the transaction."

(This is to describe the many phases involved in the house-selling process to let the Client know you know what you are doing.)

Agent: *"In addition to these particular duties, my real estate agent knowledge and resources will help you sell your house more successfully and efficiently. For example, I am well-versed in the local market and the demands of buyers and sellers. I can utilize this expertise to assist you in making educated decisions about how to price and advertise your house."*

(This is to emphasize the value of your expertise and resources.)

Agent: *"I also have a network of industry specialists and a track record of successful sales to assist you in selling your house faster and more efficiently. For example, I might be able to put you in touch with possible purchasers or recommend you to other specialists who can assist you with certain areas of the sale process."*

(This explains the importance of your network and relationships and how they have favorably affected your sales.)

Agent: *"I recognize that you have options when it comes to choosing an agent, and I would be happy to gain your business. My experience, skill, and devotion to my clients make me the greatest choice for you, in my opinion. I hope you will give me the opportunity to show it to you."*

(The last section requests the opportunity to call them to action to strike a deal with you.)

70. THIS OFFER IS TOO LOW; WE REQUIRE ADDITIONAL FUNDS.

This is the objection you will often face when a seller is not comfortable with the offer that is available for their home. They actually do not know much about how the real estate market works, so when you bring in an offer for them, and it is way below their expectation, it is very likely that they will come back with this type of objection.

If you want to handle that objection with ease, then this script will do the magic:

Agent: *"I realize that you want to receive the greatest price for your property, and I absolutely agree that setting a high goal is essential. However, you must also analyze the present market circumstances as well as the specifics of the offer you have received."*

(This will help acknowledge the client's wish to receive more money for their house and emphasize the need to consider market conditions.)

Agent: *"Based on my study of the local market and your home's qualities, I feel the offer price is appropriate and represents the current demand for properties like yours. The location, condition, and qualities of the property, as well as the general market circumstances, can all have an impact on the price of a home."*

(This is to provide a market analysis and explain why the offer price is what it is.)

Agent: *"While it's normal to want to hold out for a greater price, it's crucial to remember that rejecting an offer means you'll miss out on the chance to sell your house. It may also imply that you must continue to pay for house maintenance, taxes, and other expenditures, which may be costly and unpleasant."*

(This is to underline the risks of rejecting the offer.)

Agent: *"If you are willing, I would be delighted to collaborate with you in attempting to negotiate a better price with the buyer. My goal is to assist you in achieving your real estate objectives and obtaining the greatest possible price for the sale of your house. I think that with my* *skills and resources, we can establish a mutually advantageous deal that fits your requirements as well as those of others."*

(The reason here is to propose to bargain with the buyer in order to reach a mutually advantageous deal.)

Take your time to analyze the current market state with your client, and you are good to go.

71. YOU HAVE ALREADY REDUCED OUR PRICING THREE TIMES, AND IT HAS YET TO SELL; HOW CAN YOU EXPECT US TO DO SO AGAIN?

Lowering the listing price can be very frustrating to the sellers and not just them to you too, but you are not as angry as they are because you know why the pricing is like that. All you need to do is ensure they also know about this.

This script makes it very easy to do that and avoid getting them angry again:

Agent: *"I appreciate that you are upset and may be doubting the idea of additional price cuts. It's quite normal to feel this way, and I want you to know that I have your best interests in mind. The decision to reduce the price of your house was not made lightly, and it was based on a careful examination of the local market as well as the specifics of your property."*

(This is to recognize the client's dissatisfaction and to explain the reasons for the price decrease.)

Agent: *"The real estate market is volatile, and there are several factors that might impact the selling of a house. Changes in the economy, borrowing rates, or competition from other listings, for example, can all impact demand for houses like yours. In this situation, market conditions and competition from other listings may have caused the original price to be too high, necessitating repeated price reductions to make your house more competitive and appealing to purchasers."*

(This is to discuss the present market circumstances and how they will affect the selling of your house.)

Agent: *"While lowering the price of your property may be tough, bear in mind that the purpose of pricing is to attract buyers and stimulate interest in your home. A reduced price may assist to distinguish your house from the competition, increasing the likelihood of a successful sale."*

(This will help to highlight the potential benefits of additional price reductions.)

Agent: *"If you are uncertain about whether to drop the price again, I would be pleased to give you further information and tools to assist you make an informed choice. This might contain a market study, current market circumstances and trends, or advice from other industry specialists. My major purpose is to assist you in achieving your real estate objectives and obtaining the greatest possible price for the sale of your house."*

(This offer provides additional information and resources to assist you in making an educated decision.)

Agent: *"I recognize that you have options when it comes to choosing an agent, and I would be happy to continue working with you to sell your property. My experience, skill, and devotion to my clients make me the greatest choice for you, in my opinion. I hope you will give me the opportunity to show it to you."*

(This is the final line that shows that you are still willing to work with them by requesting the opportunity to continue working with you.)

This is one of the most difficult objections most realtors have faced. However, it has an easy solution. Put yourself in your client's shoes and feel their pain. Then educate them on why you took those actions and the gain in taking these actions. Take your time to do so and gain their trust again.

72. WE HAVE A ONE-OF-A-KIND HOME, BUT THE BUYER HAS YET TO COME THROUGH.

If you practice using the patterns, you can address practically any issue. Never, ever, ever use the word "but" since it essentially informs the prospect that they are incorrect. Most of my customers bring up that same topic shortly before they list their properties,

And this is a script you can use to tell them about how you have been working on getting their home sold:

Agent: *"I understand your frustration that your one-of-a-kind home has failed to sell, and I entirely agree that finding the appropriate buyer for a unique property like yours is critical. Marketing a one-of-a-kind home can be difficult since it necessitates a different strategy than marketing a more standard property."*

(This will show that you recognize the client's unhappiness and underline the necessity of properly selling a distinctive house.)

Agent: *"As your real estate agent, I've taken a number of efforts to properly advertise your house, including using high-quality images and virtual tours to highlight the features and benefits of your home: Making use of social media and internet channels to reach a larger audience, Hosting open houses and other activities to build interest and attract purchasers."*

(This outlines the procedures you took to promote the house properly.)

Agent: *"In addition to these targeted marketing efforts, my experience and skills as a real estate agent may assist in ensuring that your house receives the attention it deserves. For example, I have a thorough awareness of the local market as well as the demands of buyers and sellers, and I can apply this expertise to personalize my approach to your home's unique needs and goals."*

(This section underlines the importance of your knowledge and resources.)

Agent: *"If you are unsure how to continue, I would be pleased to give you further information and resources to assist you in making an informed decision. This might contain a market study, current market circumstances and trends, or advice from other industry specialists. My major purpose is to assist you in achieving your real estate objectives and obtaining the greatest possible price for the sale of your house."*

(This offer provides additional information and resources to assist your client (s) in making an educated decision.)

Agent: *"I am aware that you have options when it comes to choosing an agent, and I would consider it an honor to continue working with you to market your special house. My experience, skill, and devotion to my clients make me the greatest choice for you, in my opinion. I hope you will give me the opportunity to show it to you."*

(This is to show your interest in working with the client requesting the opportunity to continue working with you.)

Special homes require special clients. Most people admire one-of-a-kind homes, but they do not take action to buy. They assume they must be expensive or maintenance cost is high, while some might think it is reserved for some class of people. This takes a professional realtor to strategize its marketing differently in a way that attracts buyers, which is what your client must realize.

73. WHERE WERE YOU WHEN I PUT MY PROPERTY ON THE MARKET?

This is another way sellers get back at realtors, especially when they did not assist in getting their home listed; there is this belief that if the realtor does not help them list their house, they won't be a perfect fit to help them sell it. Try to be calm and apologize for not helping them.

By using this script, you should let them realize that transactions go beyond listing and that there is so much more a professional realtor can still offer them:

Agent: *"I realize that you may be dissatisfied and wondering why I was unable to assist you when your home was on the market. I'm sorry I couldn't help you at the time, and I understand if you were disappointed."*

(This is to recognize the client's displeasure and apologize for being unable to assist sooner.)

Agent: *"There might be various reasons why I couldn't assist you sooner, including my schedule is completely booked and my inability to take on further customers.*

I may not have been familiar with the specifics of your house or the local market circumstances, so I may not have been able to deliver the kind of care and attention you need."

(This explains the reasons that prevented you from being able to assist sooner.)

Agent: *"Regardless of why I was unable to assist you earlier, I feel that my skills and resources as a real estate agent may make a significant difference in the selling of your house. I understand the local market and the needs of buyers and sellers, and I have a track record of effectively promoting and selling homes for my clients. In addition to my professional credentials, I am dedicated to providing excellent customer service and collaborating closely with my clients to ensure their requirements and goals are realized."*

(This is to underline the importance of your knowledge and resources in getting their home sold.)

Agent: *"I recognize that you have options when it comes to choosing an agent, and I would be happy to gain your business. My experience, skill, and devotion to my clients make me the greatest choice for you, in my opinion. I hope you will give me the opportunity to show it to you."*

(This is to request the opportunity to gain their trust again and handle the sales of their home again.)

Calm your clients and show them what you have to offer that sparks excellence.

74. I HAVE TO KEEP MY PROMISE TO THE AGENT I ORIGINALLY BOUGHT THE HOME WITH

This is one of the largest financial decisions your client will make, and you want it to be a wise decision for them, not something made on emotion. You want them to be as knowledgeable as possible to receive the greatest deal for themselves and their family.

Getting them to see many viewpoints and doing what is best for them and their family is a wise business choice. You also have to let them know that going with someone because you know them does not guarantee that you will obtain the greatest financial outcomes.

So here is the script that will help you do that with ease:

Agent: *"I understand that you have a strong relationship with your original agent and that you feel a sense of loyalty to them. It's natural that you want to maintain your word to them, and I appreciate your decision. At the same time, I feel it is critical to examine your home's* *individual requirements and goals, as well as current market conditions, when selecting an agent."*

(This is to appreciate the client's devotion to their initial agency and to convey the benefits of working with a local market expert.)

Agent: *"As a real estate agent who understands the local market and the needs of buyers and sellers, I feel I can offer a level of experience and resources that can assist you in selling your house more successfully and quickly. For example, I have a proven track record of successful sales and a network of industry specialists who can assist you in ensuring that your house receives the attention it deserves."*

(This is to underline the importance of your knowledge and resources in getting them the best offer.)

Agent: *"If you are unsure whether to work with me, I would be pleased to give you further details and resources to aid in your decision-making. This might contain a market study, current market circumstances and trends, or advice from other industry specialists. My major purpose is to assist you in achieving your real estate objectives and obtaining the greatest possible price for the sale of your house."*

(This offer provides additional information and resources to assist you in making an educated decision.)

Agent: *"I recognize that you have options when it comes to choosing an agent, and I would be happy to gain your business. My experience, skill, and devotion to my clients make me the greatest choice for you,* *in my opinion. I hope you will give me the opportunity to show it to you."*

(This is to request the opportunity to gain their business and call them to strike a deal with you.)

Most clients do this based on emotion, and you can convince them that decisions made out of emotions are not the best in real estate

75. WHEN MARKET VALUES RISE, I PLAN TO SELL MY HOUSE.

This circumstance exists if a prospect has a condition to sell their home fast. If the housing market is affected by high mortgage rates and rising home prices, it may not be the best time to sell their property, and they may wind up earning a lesser price for their house or having difficulty finding a buyer. If market circumstances improve, such as mortgage rates falling or house prices leveling off, selling their property may sound nice, but regardless you have to let them know about the risk behind selling late.

This script will show you how you will go about it:

Agent: *"I realize that you want to receive the greatest price for your property, and I absolutely agree that setting a high goal is essential. However, while deciding on the optimum time to sell, it's also crucial to examine the current market circumstances as well as the specifics of your house."*

(The purpose of this is to offer a market analysis and explain the aspects that might affect the value of a house.)

Agent: *"Based on my research of the local market and your home's qualities, I feel that now is an excellent time to sell. The location, condition, and qualities of the property, as well as the broader market circumstances, can all have an impact on the value of a house. While it is true that market prices change over time, it is also crucial to remember that there are numerous aspects that can affect a home's worth, and it can be impossible to forecast when values will rise."*

(This is to appreciate the client's wish to receive the best potential price for their house and to emphasize the need to consider current market conditions.)

Agent: *"While it may be tempting to wait for market prices to rise before selling your house, it's vital to remember that there are hazards to doing so. For example, you may have to continue paying for house maintenance, taxes, and other bills, which may be costly and unpleasant. Furthermore, the longer you wait to sell, the more competition you may encounter from other listings, which can affect your home's price and demand."*

(This is to highlight the possible hazards of waiting to sell.)

Agent: *"If you are unsure whether to sell now or wait for market values to rise, I would be delighted to give you further information and tools to assist you in making an informed decision. This might contain a market study and current market information."*

(This offer provides additional information and resources to assist you in making an educated decision.)

Explain the current market circumstances to your client and be honest in telling them if this objection will be a good decision depending on the current market situation.

76. WE WISH TO POSTPONE THE SALE.

If a house has been on the market for a long time and no one has made an offer, the seller may become disheartened.

Perhaps they have spent a lot of money on house advertising and made several price reductions, yet no one calls. However, their house may eventually become an expired listing since there are still things you can do if their house doesn't sell.

All you need to do is use this script, making it much more manageable.

Agent: *"I realize you have opted to postpone the sale of your property, and I respect your decision. It's natural to want to thoroughly analyze your alternatives and ensure that you're making the greatest decision for your family and future. However, bear in mind that the real estate market is continuously changing, and understanding current market circumstances and how they may affect the value and demand for your house may be beneficial."*

(This is to accept the client's decision to wait and emphasize the necessity of considering current market circumstances.)

Agent: *"Based on my research of the local market and your home's qualities, I feel that now is an excellent time to sell. The location, condition, and qualities of the property, as well as the broader market circumstances, can all have an impact on the value of a house. While* *it is true that market prices change over time, it is also crucial to remember that there are numerous aspects that can affect a home's worth, and it can be impossible to forecast when values will rise."*

(The purpose of this is to offer a market analysis obtained from your research and explain the aspects that might affect the value of a house.)

Agent: *"While it may be tempting to wait to sell your house, it is vital to remember that there are hazards to doing so. For example, you may have to continue paying for house maintenance, taxes, and other bills, which may be costly and unpleasant. Furthermore, the longer you wait to sell, the more competition you may encounter from other listings, which can affect your home's price and demand."*

(This is to highlight the possible hazards of waiting to sell.)

Agent: *"If you are unsure whether to sell now or wait, I would be delighted to give you more information and tools to assist you in making an informed decision. This might contain a market study, current market circumstances and trends, or advice from other industry specialists. My major purpose is to assist you in achieving your real estate objectives and obtaining the greatest possible price for the sale of your house."*

(This offer provides additional information and resources to assist you in making an educated decision.)

77. HOW LONG HAVE YOU BEEN IN THE REAL ESTATE BUSINESS?

What your prospect wants here is information. They want to know your experience, and you should start by telling them your educational background and why you possess the qualities of a realtor. Tell them about the challenges of your career and the lessons you have learned so far.

Then mention your achievements so far and how you have handled properties similar to theirs. You can then tell them how you stay up to date with the current trends in the real estate field, and keep updated with the current market.

If you do not have much experience, be honest but prove to them that you are knowledgeable enough to handle the business and show them the few successful transactions you have done.

Here is a script that you might use to deal with the objection

Agent: *"Thank you for inquiring about my real estate expertise and credentials. I've been selling real estate for [so and so number of years], and I know the local market and the needs of buyers and sellers. In addition to my professional experience, I have considerable training and many qualifications and designations that reflect my knowledge in the sector."*

(This is to respond to the client's inquiry and offer a quick outline of your expertise and qualifications.)

Agent: *"While it is true that experience is a significant component to consider when choosing a real estate agent, I feel that the value of an agent's knowledge and resources should also be considered. As a real*

estate agent, I have access to a variety of tools and services that can assist me in marketing and selling your house in a more successful and efficient manner. Professional networks, market analysis tools, and a range of marketing methods and approaches are among the resources available to assist you get your house in front of the right purchasers."

(This is to underline the importance of your knowledge and resources in selling their home as quickly as possible.)

Agent: *"In addition to my professional experience and qualifications, I've had the chance to deal with a diverse set of customers and assist them in achieving their real estate objectives. For example, I have successfully [talk about examples of your triumphs and how you have assisted your clients, such as "sold properties for top dollar," "negotiated successful agreements," "assisted first-time purchasers through the process," and so on]. These accomplishments, I feel, reflect my ability to deliver great service and to collaborate closely with my clients to ensure their requirements and goals are realized."*

(This section aims to share instances of your triumphs and how you have assisted your clients.)

Agent: *"I recognize that you have options when it comes to choosing an agent, and I would be happy to gain your business. My experience, skill, and devotion to my clients make me the greatest choice for you, in my opinion. I hope you will give me the opportunity to show it to you."*

(This is to request the opportunity to gain their business trust and also proceed to make a deal with them.)

78. OUR BANK'S LOAN MODIFICATION (PRE-FORECLOSURE/NED) IS STILL IN THE WORKS AND HAS NOT BEEN COMPLETED.

Today's market is highly competitive, and integrating premarketing to mitigate listing presentation problems merely makes sense. What you need to do here is to let them know what they would have to lose if the price was right and the situation couldn't be passed up. It would help if you made them understand they may miss out on the best time to sell their house.

This script will show you how to do that strategically:

Agent: *"I realize you are negotiating a loan modification with the bank and that you may be facing pre-foreclosure or NED. I can understand that this is a difficult and stressful moment for you, and I want to reassure you that I am here to assist, support, and guide you during the process."*

(This is to acknowledge the client's predicament and indicate that you realize the difficulties they are experiencing.)

Agent: *"Even if you are working with the bank on a loan modification or are facing the prospect of a pre-foreclosure or NED, there are various solutions that may be available to assist you in selling your house. You may be able to [talk about choices such as "short sale" or "sell to an investor"] your property, for example. These choices may enable you to sell your property and maybe prevent foreclosure, which can harm your credit and financial circumstances."*

(This is to discuss the possibilities available to assist them in selling their house.)

Agent: *"As a real estate agent, I am well-versed in the local market and the demands of buyers and sellers, and I have worked with customers in comparable situations in the past. I can give you the knowledge and tools you need to navigate the process and make the best option for your circumstances."*

(This is to underline the importance of your knowledge and resources.)

Agent: *"I recognize that you have options when it comes to choosing an agent, and I would be happy to gain your business. My experience, skill, and devotion to my clients make me the greatest choice for you, in my opinion. I hope you will give me the opportunity to show it to you."*

(This is to request the opportunity to gain their business.)

79. HOW WELL DO YOU MARKET YOUR LISTINGS? I WANT MY LISTING TO GET A LOT OF EXPOSURE.

This objection always pops up when concerns about advertising exist. Most of the time, the client does not understand the distinction between active and passive marketing. Simply enough, passive marketing involves waiting impatiently for a buyer to come along and purchase your house.

On the other side, active marketing is significantly more aggressive and more predictable. So you have to tell them how you advertise your listing to produce the best outreach and result that will satisfy them.

Here is a response to the question,

Agent: *"I entirely understand that you want a lot of promotion for your property. The process of selling a home involves a lot of marketing, so it's critical to create a strategy that will effectively reach your target market and produce the greatest results."*

(This is to accept that the client wants a lot of advertising and to emphasize the value of creating a focused marketing strategy.)

Agent: *"I have a variety of tools and resources at my disposal as a real estate agent to market properties and connect with prospective purchasers. Online marketing tools, social media, print ads, email marketing, open houses, and other methods may be among them. I collaborate with my customers to create a marketing strategy that is specific to their needs and objectives and makes use of the best available tools and resources to target the correct audience."*

(This is to describe your marketing strategy and the resources and methods you employ to market properties.)

Agent: *"In order to get the best results, the marketing strategy needs to be customized for the particular home and the neighborhood market. This might entail showcasing the property's distinctive qualities and amenities, focusing on a certain buyer demographic, and taking advantage of regional market trends and circumstances. I am dedicated to creating a marketing strategy that is specific to your* *demands and objectives since I have a thorough awareness of the local market and the needs of buyers and sellers."*

(This justifies the significance of adjusting the marketing strategy to the unique property and the local market.)

Agent: *"I have the skills and resources you need to realize your real estate objectives as an experienced and devoted real estate agent. I am dedicated to giving my customers the finest service and representation possible since I have a thorough awareness of the local market and the needs of buyers and sellers. My knowledge and commitment make me the greatest person to assist you in achieving your real estate objectives".*

(To underscore the importance of dealing with a knowledgeable and committed real estate agent.)

80. SINCE NONE OF YOUR LISTINGS FOR HOMES FALL INSIDE OUR BUDGET, HOW WILL YOU MANAGE OUR DEMAND?

This top-seller objection mainly focuses on the agent's lack of expertise in a particular price range. You might sell people homes for much more or less than they would hope to get for their own house.

So the clients frequently move up to your price range after you sell their properties, contrary to your regular practice of selling homes in lower price ranges. So it may stand to you that starting to sell items in your price range would be their next natural step.

You can use the following script to respond to the criticism :

Agent: *"You're worried about the pricing range of the homes I work with, and I entirely get that. I have experience working with customers in a number of pricing ranges and it is normal for agents to work with properties in a range of price points."*

(This is to acknowledge the client's worry regarding the price range and to clarify that working with houses at various price ranges is not unusual for agents.)

Agent: *"I have experience working with properties in a variety of price ranges, and as a real estate expert, I have a thorough awareness of the neighborhood market and the requirements of both buyers and sellers. Regardless of the property's price range, I have a proven track record of success in assisting my customers in achieving their real estate objectives."*

(This describes your background and specialization in dealing with homes at various price levels.)

Agent: *"I have the skills and resources you need to accomplish your real estate objectives because I am a committed and seasoned real estate agent. I am dedicated to giving my customers the finest service and representation possible since I have a thorough awareness of the local market and the needs of buyers and sellers. Regardless of the property's price range, I firmly think that my knowledge and commitment make me the greatest choice to assist you in achieving your real estate objectives."*

(This justification explains the advantages of dealing with a knowledgeable, committed real estate agent.)

Agent: *"I would be pleased to give you further details about my experience and area of specialization. I may offer you references from previous clients, case studies, or other data that illustrates my capacity to assist buyers and sellers in a range of price ranges to realize their real estate objectives. Let's collaborate to create a solution that satisfies your requirements and enables you to accomplish your real estate objectives."*

(This is to conclude by showing interest in giving them more details if they need them and also showing your interest in collaborating with them and striking a deal.)

81. I NEED AN EXACT NET AMOUNT TO MOVE BECAUSE I CAN'T AFFORD TO BUY A NEW HOME IF I TAKE A LOSS, AND I ALSO NEED TO START MY NEW JOB WITHIN 90 DAYS.

When an objection like this comes up, all you have to do is let them know that nobody will provide them with the net amount they require to make this move. You have to make them know you have also been in difficult situations like theirs.

Here's a script you could use to deal with the objection

Agent: *"I completely understand that you need to net a certain amount in order to move and that you have a deadline to meet. To achieve the best possible result, it is critical to carefully consider all of the factors that can affect the sale of your property."*

(This is to acknowledge the client's concern about netting a specific amount and explain the importance of considering all of the factors that can affect the sale of the property.)

Agent: *"As a real estate professional, I have a thorough understanding of the specific market and the needs of buyers and sellers, and I apply that knowledge to create a pricing and marketing strategy tailored to your specific needs and goals. My goal is to assist you in obtaining the highest possible sale price for your property while also taking into account the timeline and other factors that are important to you."*

(This is to describe your pricing and marketing strategy for the property.)

Agent: *"I do have resources and expertise you need to achieve your real estate goals as an experienced and dedicated real estate agent. I have a thorough understanding of the local market and the needs of buyers and sellers, and I am dedicated to providing my clients with the best service and representation possible. My skills and devotion, I feel, make me the perfect candidate to assist you reach your real estate goals, regardless of the timetable or other restrictions you may be facing."*

(This is why working with an experienced and dedicated real estate agent is beneficial.)

Agent: *"I would be pleased to offer you with further information about my approach to pricing and promoting your home, or if you have any special issues or questions. I can also investigate potential solutions or strategies that may be able to assist you in meeting your objectives within the timeframe you have set. Let us collaborate to find a solution."*

(This is to offer more information about your approach and to explore potential solutions.)

82. IF THAT'S THE LAST PRICE YOU'LL ACCEPT FOR THE PROPERTY, I'LL HAVE TO SELL IT MYSELF.

When clients give this objection, they also claim that they can generate more competition through the brokerage community. This is one of the most typical complaints raised by potential homeowners seeking a Real Estate Agent alternative. The homeowners are attempting to save money by selling their properties themselves, So how do you go about this? This is how you go about:

Agent: *"I fully understand that you are concerned about the sale price of your property. To get the greatest potential result, it is critical to thoroughly analyze all of the elements that might affect the selling of your house."*

(This is to recognize the client's worry regarding the sale price and to emphasize the need to consider all of the elements that might influence the sale of the property.)

Agent: *"As a real estate expert, I have a thorough awareness of the local market and the needs of buyers and sellers, and I apply that knowledge to create a pricing and marketing plan targeted to your specific needs and goals. My goal is to assist you in obtaining the highest possible sale price for your property while also taking into account the other factors that are important to you."*

(This is to describe your price and marketing strategy for the property.)

Agent: *"I have the expertise and resources you need to reach your real estate objectives as an experienced and devoted real estate agent. I have a thorough awareness of the local market and the needs of*

buyers and sellers, and I am dedicated to providing my clients with the finest service and representation available. I believe that my experience and dedication make me the best choice to assist you in achieving your real estate objectives."

(This emphasizes the importance of dealing with an experienced and professional real estate agent.)

Agent: *"I would be pleased to offer you with further information about my approach to pricing and promoting your home, or if you have any special issues or questions. I can also investigate potential solutions or strategies that may be able to assist you in achieving your objectives. Let's collaborate to find a solution that meets your needs while also assisting you in achieving your real estate goals."*

(This is to share additional information about your approach and to explore potential solutions.)

83. IF WE ARE SELLING IT AT THAT LOW PRICE, WE WOULD RATHER SELL IT OURSELVES AND PAY YOU 3% TO THE REALTOR WHO ASSISTS US IN DOING SO

The truth is that you are well-versed in today's market and have the most in-depth understanding of what can make or break a deal. In a real estate transaction, you have to ensure that your client doesn't want to leave money on the table, and using an experienced agent can help ensure that doesn't happen; usually, when you are selling at a low price, they are due to some valid reason which you will need to explain to them. So how do you explain this?

Here is a script that you could use:

Agent: *"I entirely appreciate that you are anxious about the sale price of your house. To get the greatest potential result, it is critical to thoroughly analyze all of the elements that might affect the selling of your house."*

(This is to recognize the client's worry regarding the sale price and to emphasize the need to consider all of the elements that might influence the sale of the property.)

Agent: *"As a real estate expert, I have a thorough awareness of the local market and the needs of buyers and sellers, and I apply that knowledge to create a pricing and marketing plan targeted to your specific needs and goals. My objective is to assist you in obtaining the highest potential sale price for your house while also taking into account the other aspects that are essential to you."*

(This is to describe your price and marketing strategy for the property.)

Agent: *"I have the expertise and resources you need to reach your real estate objectives as an experienced and devoted real estate agent. I have a thorough awareness of the local market and the needs of buyers and sellers, and I am dedicated to providing my clients with the finest service and representation available. I feel that my experience and devotion make me the greatest candidate to assist you in achieving your real estate objectives."*

(This emphasizes the importance of dealing with an experienced and professional real estate agent.)

Agent: *"I would be pleased to offer you with further information about my approach to pricing and promoting your home, or if you have any special issues or questions. I may also investigate prospective solutions or methods that may be able to assist you in achieving your objectives. Let's collaborate to develop a solution that matches your demands while also assisting you in achieving your real estate goals."*

(This is to share additional information about your approach and to explore potential solutions.)

Agent: *"I hear that you are exploring the option of selling the property yourself and paying 3% to the agent who sells it. While this may be a viable option in some cases, it is critical to carefully consider all of the factors that may affect the sale of your property, including the value of the services provided by a real estate agent. As an experienced and dedicated real estate agent, I provide a variety of services to assist you in obtaining the best possible sale price for your property, such as marketing and advertising, negotiations, and contract management. These services can assist you in achieving a higher sale price and a quicker sale, which may more than offset the cost of my commission. Let's collaborate to investigate all of your options and find the best solution for you."*

(This addresses the client's concern about paying a 3% commission to the agent who sells the property.)

84. WE WANT TO AVOID A LISTING PRICE THAT WILL GET IT SOLD IN A WEEK.

You have to let them know that you will work with them to get the best possible price for their home, and since they created that objection themselves, you are not going to handle it and would instead turn down ten offers than never receive one. The idea is to prompt them and make them aware of the effect of their actions.

Here's a script you could use to explain that:

Agent: *"I completely understand that you are concerned about the timeline for selling your property. It's essential to carefully consider all the factors that can affect the sale of your property to achieve the best possible outcome".*

(This is to acknowledge the client's concern about the sale timeline and explain the importance of considering all of the factors that can affect the sale of the property.)

Agent: *"As a real estate expert, I have a thorough awareness of the local market and the needs of buyers and sellers, and I apply that knowledge to create a pricing and marketing plan targeted to your specific needs and goals. My goal is to assist you in achieving the best possible sale price for your property while also considering the timeline and other important factors."*

(This is to describe your price and marketing strategy for the property.)

Agent: *"I have the expertise and resources you need to reach your real estate objectives as an experienced and devoted real estate agent. I have a thorough awareness of the local market and the needs of*

buyers and sellers, and I am dedicated to providing my clients with the finest service and representation available. My skills and devotion, I feel, make me the perfect candidate to assist you reach your real estate goals, regardless of the timetable or other restrictions you may be facing."

(This is why working with an experienced and professional real estate agent is beneficial.)

Agent: *"I would be pleased to offer you with further information about my approach to pricing and promoting your home, or if you have any special issues or questions. I may also investigate prospective solutions or tactics that may be able to assist you in meeting your objectives within the timeframe you have set. Let's collaborate to develop a solution that matches your demands while also assisting you in achieving your real estate goals."*

(This is to share additional information about your approach and to explore potential solutions.)

85. WE MAY ALWAYS LOWER THE PRICE LATER.

Most Sellers believe that until they reduce their Home sales, they won't sell. These Objections are usually best cleared in your listing presentation, which should be directed back to your presentation, where you display surrounding homes that have previously sold for comparable prices to the market analysis.

Here's a script you may employ to explain that:

Agent: *"I understand you are considering offering your house at a higher price and then lowering it later if required. While this may be* *a realistic choice in certain situations, it is critical to thoroughly analyze all of the aspects that may influence the sale of your home in order to obtain the best potential result."*

(This is to recognize the client's worry regarding the sale price and to emphasize the need to consider all of the elements that might influence the sale of the property.)

Agent: *"As a real estate expert, I have a thorough awareness of the local market and the needs of buyers and sellers, and I apply that knowledge to create a pricing and marketing plan targeted to your specific needs and goals. My objective is to assist you in obtaining the highest potential sale price for your house while also taking into account the other aspects that are essential to you."*

(This is to describe your price and marketing strategy for the property.)

Agent: *"While it may appear to be a smart idea to advertise your house at a higher price and then lower it if required, there are some possible downsides to this strategy. For example, if the property is overvalued, it may not appeal to potential purchasers and may remain on the market for a lengthy amount of time. This can be irritating and upsetting for you, and it may ultimately result in a reduced sale price. By appropriately valuing your home from the beginning, you may be able to attract more serious bidders and accomplish a speedier sale at a better price."*

(This demonstrates the possible disadvantages of the "come down in price later" technique.)

Agent: *"I would be pleased to offer you with further information about my approach to pricing and promoting your home, or if you have any special issues or questions. I may also investigate prospective solutions or methods that may be able to assist you in achieving your objectives. Let's collaborate to develop a solution that matches your demands while also assisting you in achieving your real estate goals."*

(This is an offer to provide more information about your approach and to explore potential solutions.)

86. IF OUR FIRM, A FRIEND, OR A NEIGHBOR WISHES TO PURCHASE OUR HOUSE, WE WOULD LIKE AN EXCLUSION IN THE LISTING CONTRACT.

This is very common with sellers. They always want a commission-free listing if their property is sold to a family or friend because they believe there won't be much negotiation and effort to sell such property.

Nevertheless, you must tell them that their personal marketing hasn't worked, so they must hire you. So they should value your services, and also you can suggest alternatives that support their opinion and have little or no adverse effect on you.

Here's a script to address the argument

Agent: *"I realize that you want an exclusion in the listing contract in case your employer, friend, or neighbor wants to buy the property, and I admire your willingness to investigate all of your choices.*

However, before making a choice, it is critical to thoroughly analyze the potential downsides of this strategy."

(This is to recognize the client's wish for a listing contract exclusion and outline this strategy's potential downsides.)

Agent: *"By leaving specific parties out of the listing contract, you may be restricting your visibility to potential purchasers and decreasing your chances of getting the greatest possible price for your home. You may also be establishing an unneeded barrier for potential purchasers who are interested in your house, which may impact your ability to sell the property quickly and efficiently."*

(This describes why specific parties should be excluded from the listing contract.)

Agent: *"While I appreciate your wish for an exclusion in the listing contract, I would be delighted to work with you to explore alternate alternatives that may meet your concerns while also increasing your visibility to possible purchasers. For example, we may include in the contract a clause that permits you to negotiate directly with any interested parties, or we could look into other solutions that could help you achieve your goals while also increasing your prospects of a successful sale. Let's collaborate to develop a solution that matches your demands while also assisting you in achieving your real estate goals."*

(This proposes collaborating with the customer to seek other options.)

87. IT IS CRUCIAL TO US THAT YOU VISIT OUR HOUSE, EVEN IF YOU DO NOT BELIEVE IT WILL AFFECT THE PRICE. WE'D WANT YOU TO VIEW IT.

Clients assume that for the agent to know the house's total value, they have to be physically present at the house. Although, you have to tell them that you realize how important visiting your house is to them, which is why you will only depend on something other than just visiting to evaluate their homes.

Here is a script that you might use to deal with the objection

Agent: *"I recognize that seeing your house is important to you, and I respect your interest in determining the best strategy to price your property. As a real estate specialist, I have a thorough awareness of the local market and the needs of buyers and sellers, and I utilize that knowledge to build a pricing plan targeted to your specific needs and objectives."*

(This is to recognize the client's wish for you to view their house and explain the benefit of your pricing strategy.)

Agent: *"My pricing strategy includes a thorough examination of the local market, including comparable sales data, market trends, and other factors that may influence the value of your home. In order to calculate the greatest potential price, I additionally analyze the particular features and aspects of your house."*

(This is to describe your pricing strategy for the property.)

Agent: *"While seeing a property in person may be beneficial for understanding its features and qualities, it is critical to thoroughly analyze all of the aspects that might affect a property's worth in order to reach the best potential. Personal views or subjective judgements about the worth of a property can be impacted by a number of variables, such as emotional connection or personal preferences, and may not correctly reflect the object's genuine value. I can assist you in determining the most accurate and reasonable price for your house by relying on a careful examination of the market and the particular attributes of your property."*

(This is to highlight the possible disadvantages of depending on human judgments regarding the worth of an item.)

Agent: *"I would be pleased to share further information about my approach to pricing your home, or if you have any special issues or questions. I can also look into various solutions or tactics that might help you reach your goals while keeping your budget and other limits in mind. Let's collaborate to develop a solution that matches your demands while also assisting you in achieving your real estate goals."*

(This is an opportunity to share more information about your approach and explore potential solutions.)

88. COULD YOU HOST OPEN HOUSES?

Most Clients need to learn that open houses do not actually get the house sold; you will have to make them understand that you will prefer the passive way of marketing which will be effective when backed up with practical steps rather than being aggressive.

Here's a script you may use to respond to the complaint:

Agent: *"I realize that you want to host open houses to advertise your home, and I admire your desire to discover the ideal marketing approach for your property. As a real estate expert, I have a thorough awareness of the local market and the needs of buyers and sellers, and I apply that knowledge to create a marketing plan targeted to your specific needs and goals."*

(This addresses the client's worry regarding open houses and conveys the benefit of your approach.)

Agent: *"My approach to promoting your home comprises a variety of activities geared to reach out to potential buyers and highlight the unique attributes of your property. This encompasses both classic marketing means like print and direct mail, as well as internet marketing via websites, social media, and other platforms. I also use my substantial real estate business network to assist advertise your home to potential purchasers."*

(The purpose of this section is to describe your approach to promoting the property.)

Agent: *"While open houses may be an excellent way to sell your home, they are not necessarily the most successful way to reach potential buyers. Open houses may not attract a significant number of serious purchasers in some circumstances, or they may not deliver the best value for your time and effort. However, alternative tactics, such as private showings or virtual tours, that I may utilize to display your home to potential purchasers may be more effective in reaching your target demographic."*

(This is to describe the possible disadvantages of open homes and how to mitigate them.)

Agent: *"I would be pleased to give you further information about my approach to promoting your home, or if you have any special reservations or questions concerning the usage of open houses. I can also look into various solutions or tactics that might help you reach your goals while keeping your budget and other limits in mind. Let's collaborate to develop a solution that matches your demands while also assisting you in achieving your real estate goals."*

(This is an invitation to share further information about your approach and to consider potential solutions.)

89. YOU DON'T APPEAR TO MARKET, YET EVERY OTHER AGENT WE SPEAK WITH SAYS THEY DO THE SAME THINGS YOU DO, INCLUDING ADVERTISING; WHY DON'T YOU ADVERTISE?

Agents who promote extensively do not want to work. So you have to let them know that these people will tell them that they actively prospect every day to impress them. It is like when those agents tell them If they could sell a property without investing 50% of their money?, which means Either they are not clever or they aren't telling you the entire truth, and that does not sound fair also that you will instead do effective passive marketing rather than aggressive marketing.

Here is a script that you might use to explain better to your clients:

Agent: *"I understand your anxiety about advertising, and I respect your desire to discover the most effective marketing approach for* *your house. As a real estate expert, I have a thorough awareness of the local market and the needs of buyers and sellers, and I apply that knowledge to create a marketing plan targeted to your specific needs and goals."*

(This is to address the client's worry about advertising and show your marketing strategy's worth.)

Agent: *"My approach to promoting your home comprises a variety of activities geared to reach out to potential buyers and highlight the unique attributes of your property. This encompasses both classic marketing means like print and direct mail, as well as internet marketing via websites, social media, and other platforms. I also use my substantial real estate business network to assist advertise your home to potential purchasers."*

(The purpose of this section is to describe your approach to promoting the property.)

Agent: *"While advertising may be an effective technique for promoting your home, it is critical to carefully analyze all of the aspects that can influence the sale of your home in order to obtain the best potential result. In certain situations, a marketing plan centered on advertising may not be the most successful way to contact potential consumers, or it may not deliver the best value for your money. I can help you reach your real estate goals in the most cost-effective and efficient way possible by carefully analyzing all of your alternatives and designing a customized marketing approach."*

(This is to demonstrate the possible disadvantages of advertising-based marketing techniques.)

Agent: *"I would be pleased to offer you with further information about my approach to promoting your home, or if you have any special issues or queries. I can also look into various solutions or tactics that might help you reach your goals while keeping your budget and other limits in mind. Let's collaborate to develop a solution that matches your demands while also assisting you in achieving your real estate goals."*

(This is an opportunity to share more information about your approach and explore potential solutions.)

90. WE DO NOT NEED TO PAY AN EXTRA $250 TRANSACTION FEE SINCE WE ARE CONFIDENT THAT THE 7% WILL COVER YOUR EXPENDITURES.

This objection is what you get when the client thinks they are paying you more than you should receive, but they do not know that not all properties sell eventually. Let them know that if not that you are a licensed specialist that tracks their transaction daily, they might lose more than $250 if no one monitors their trade regularly.

Here is a script that you might use to deal with the objection.

Agent: *"I entirely understand that you are concerned about the expenses involved with my services. To get the greatest potential result, it is critical to thoroughly analyze all of the elements that might affect the selling of your house."*

(This is to address the client's concerns regarding pricing and convey the value of your services.)

Agent: *"As a real estate expert, I have a thorough awareness of the local market and the needs of buyers and sellers, and I apply that knowledge to create a pricing and marketing plan targeted to your specific needs and goals. My objective is to assist you in obtaining the highest potential sale price for your house while also taking into account the other aspects that are essential to you."*

(This is to describe your price and marketing strategy for the property.)

Agent: *"I have the expertise and resources you need to reach your real estate objectives as an experienced and devoted real estate agent. I have a thorough awareness of the local market and the needs of buyers and sellers, and I am dedicated to providing my clients with the finest service and representation available. Regardless of the costs you may be paid, I think that my skill and devotion make me the greatest choice to assist you in achieving your real estate goals."*

(This emphasizes the importance of dealing with an experienced and professional real estate agent.)

Agent: *"I would be pleased to share further information about my approach to pricing and promoting your home, or if you have any special issues or questions regarding the fees connected with my services. I can also look into various solutions or tactics that might help you reach your goals while keeping your budget and other limits in mind. Let's collaborate to develop a solution that matches your demands while also assisting you in achieving your real estate goals."*

(This is an opportunity to share more information about your approach and explore potential solutions.)

BOTH SELLERS AND BUYERS OBJECTIONS

91. WE ARE UNABLE TO PAY A COMMISSION.

This is a typical criticism, and it stems from the fact that not all clients can afford to pay your commission, and some clients might feel that a commission is unnecessary because they believe the seller should rather pay the commission. The same thing applies to sellers; if a realtor is not careful, the realtor might gain little or nothing. Buyers might become reluctant after paying a lot of fees to purchase and inspect the property, while sellers want to hold on to as much gain as possible.

Most of the time, the solution is to explain to them that the commission is justifiable and negotiable(if you are willing to negotiate). You must be ready to tell them precisely what you do and how strenuous it might be. Let them know how much time you spend, ensuring the transaction is legit.

Explain to them what you use the commission for. Let the clients know that taxes are to be paid, your staff members, the documentation you do, and so on, require considerable money. Finally, show them evidence of your past successes and testimonials from previous clients. Try to show them they might not have a smooth transaction if a realtor is not involved.

This is a way of telling a reluctant client how important you are to the transaction and to justify every penny you collect. Here is a script that can be of help.

Agent: *"I understand your concern regarding the cost of employing an agent. Purchasing a home is a significant financial commitment, and it is natural to want to save money whenever possible."*

(This statement acknowledges their worry and empathizes with them; this will reassure them that you are on the same page.)

Agent: *"While it is true that employing an agent entails paying a commission, there are several advantages to doing so. For starters, an agent has access to a large number of listings and can assist you in finding the ideal property within your price range. They are also well-versed in the local real estate market and can advise you on the best bid to make and negotiate on your behalf. An agent may save you time, stress, and possibly even money in the long run."*

(This is to explain the importance of hiring a real estate agent, more specifically, to inform them what they will get if they hire or work with you.)

Agent: *"If the commission expense is an issue for you, we have a few alternatives to explore. One possibility is that I work with you on a lower commission basis. You might also pay a flat fee for my services* *rather than a portion of the sale price. Alternatively, if you want, we might consider additional innovative collaboration methods that match your goals and budget."*

(This is to provide them with different methods they may use to make working with you easier.)

Agent: *"To recap, employing a real estate agent may save you time, worry, and possibly even money in the long run. It's an investment in your future house, and I think it's worthwhile to think about. Are you willing to go through these possibilities further and discover a solution that works for you?"*

(To summarize the benefits of hiring an agent and solicit their commitment.)

Remember to pay close attention to the client's concerns and adjust your response accordingly. It's important to be understanding and flexible while emphasizing the benefits of using a real estate agent.

92. WE WILL CONTINUE TO WORK WITH OUR AGENCY.

There are several reasons why a client might want to stick to an agency. It is the same reason why people stick to certain friends. It might just be loyalty, or they might have trusted the agency because they have done a couple of successful deals. It might also be that they do not trust your agency yet and do not want to try a new agency.

What these clients usually need is the time! Give them ample time to study your agency and have more fruitful interactions with your agency before they can trust you fully to transact with your agency.

Introduce your agency to them and tell them what your agency might do for them differently to help buyers purchase a better home at a cheaper rate or to help sellers sell their houses at a more rewarding rate.

It is, however, important that you are not desperate to transact with them and accept their choices so they will understand you have their best interest in mind. Here is a script that could be of help.

Agent: *"I understand your decision to continue working with your present agent, and I appreciate your consideration. I hope you have a wonderful time with them."*

(This is to accept their choice and thank them for considering you; this shows that you appreciate their decision.)

Agent: *"Can you tell me why you decided to stick with your existing agent? I'm always searching for ways to grow and learn, and your opinion might be quite beneficial."*

(You are requesting more information about their choice now that you have demonstrated that you appreciate their decision.)

Agent: *"Even though we will not be collaborating on this transaction, I would like to be a resource for you in the future. Please contact me if you have any questions or need assistance with real estate in the region. I'm always willing to assist."*

(By offering to be a resource in the future, you are encouraging them to look beyond the current contract by portraying yourself as someone who will be extremely beneficial in the near future.)

Agent: *"I wish you the best of success with your current agent and hope you have a pleasant experience. Thank you for taking the time to consider me, and I hope to hear from you again in the future."*

(To leave the talk in a nice and pleasant tone with no red flags raised against you.)

Remember to be cordial and professional even if the customer decides not to work with you. You never know when you might get the chance to work with them again or when they might suggest friends or family to you.

93. WHAT IS YOUR COMMISSION? YOU MIGHT HAVE TO REDUCE IT.

This is where you need all the confidence you have got. You will work hard to ensure the transaction is successful with no problems, and so you deserve every gain you have in mind. However, you must be logical about the amount you collect as a commission and ensure that it follows the real estate guidelines for your country. For example, in the United States, the commission is usually between 5 - 10 percent which the buyer and seller agents split evenly.

Real estate commission also depends on how strenuous the transaction will go, the number of homes available to you as an agent, the amount your real estate firm collects (if you are working for a firm), your years of expertise as a realtor and the antitrust laws in your country. The National Association of Realtors(NAR) recommends that a realtor should not charge less than 5%.

This script will help you understand how to state your commission to your client very convincingly.

Agent: *"Thank you for inquiring about my commission. It's a crucial factor to consider when selecting an agent, and I'm pleased to go over it with you."*

(This is to acknowledge their inquiry and thank them for their interest in your services.)

Agent: *"As a real estate agent, I get compensated based on the property's sale price. The commission is often a percentage of the selling price, distributed equally between the buyer's and seller's agents. In most circumstances, the seller pays the fee, although the buyer might negotiate with the seller to cover some or all of the commission."*

(This is to describe how your commission works in the simplest and most understandable way possible.)

Agent: *"My typical commission is X%, and I'm delighted to discuss this more with you. If you have a certain budget in mind, I'm also willing to look at other commission systems. We might, for example, propose a flat fee agreement or a lower commission rate. The essential thing is to discover a solution that suits you and your requirements."*

(This is to offer additional information about your unique commission structure, more like a full discussion of several commission structure choices.)

Agent: *"While it is true that employing an agent entails paying a commission, there are several advantages to doing so. An agent can* *save you time, stress, and money in the long run. They have access to a large number of listings and can assist you in finding the ideal house for your budget. They are also well-versed in the local real estate market and can advise you on the best bid to make and negotiate on your behalf."*

(To underline the importance of working with a real estate agent like yourself and the benefits you bring.)

When discussing your commission, remember to be open to bargaining and truthful. It's critical to underscore the importance of having an agent and how they may save the client time, worry, and possibly even money in the long run.

94. WE ALREADY HAVE A REPRESENTATIVE IN MIND.

Clients who have been dealing in real estate for a long time usually might state this objection as the reason why they do not want you to represent them.

Ensure you do not argue against them as most clients will become suspicious that you are only doing that for your gains.

You should rather have a conversation about the prospective client's current experience with sales and purchase of properties. By doing so, you will realize what their pain points are and you will know how to convince that prospect to choose you as their agent.

Questions like 'what challenges have you faced so far in the purchase(or sales) of landed properties?' will help a lot to establish a goal-oriented communication between you and your prospective client.

Here is a conversation on how to deal with the argument "we already have an agent in mind":

Agent: *"I understand you've already decided to work with another agent, and I appreciate you taking the time to consider me. I hope you have a wonderful time with them."*

(This is to acknowledge their decision, thank them for considering you, and be truthful by informing you.)

Agent: *"Can you tell me why you choose to work with this specific agent? I'm always searching for ways to grow and learn, and your opinion might be quite beneficial."*

(To inquire for additional information about what the other Realtor promised to accomplish for them while also positioning yourself as an open-minded realtor rather than the stalker realtor.)

Agent: *"Even though we will not be collaborating on this transaction, I would like to be a resource for you in the future. Please contact me if you have any questions or need assistance with real estate in the region. I'm always willing to assist."*

(This is to offer to be a resource in the future; most realtors make the mistake of ending the benefits they have to give to the client once they know that the transaction is not theirs. You should not make that mistake.)

Agent: *"I wish you the best of success with your selected agent and hope you have a pleasant experience. Thank you for taking the time to consider me, and I hope to hear from you again in the future."*

(This is to end the conversation on a positive note and also help you have a place in their mind whenever they need another agent or when things do not turn out how they aspire to be with the other agent.)

Remember to be cordial and professional even if the customer decides not to work with you. You never know when you might get the chance to work with them again or when they might suggest friends or family to you.

95. CAN I CALL YOU AGAIN?

Here is another common objection. There are only two reasons for a potential client to raise this objection. The first reason could be that they give a reason to put you off without wanting to take the negotiations further. This usually happens if this is your first time introducing your agency to anyone.

Do not say, 'Okay then, I will call you next month, or I will be expecting your call. It's futile as most of them wish you would forget, or they might not allow you to talk to them anymore. Tell them that you do not wish to interrupt them, but they can briefly state any challenge they are facing regarding real estate and, in a few words, say how you can help them solve the challenges.

You can then arrange a proper time when the potential client will be free to discuss how to solve the problem further. By doing so, you have engraved yourself in the heart of the potential client as a realtor who is not only concerned about their pocket but willing to help clients.

The second reason is they might be genuinely interested in your offers, but they might have valid reasons to postpone the call. There is only one answer to this objection! Establish a solid conversation! Ask them why they are not ready yet and ensure you sound a note of urgency and further enumerate why that property is the best for your potential client at that very moment. You can honestly tell him that the price might go up later or that someone else is eyeing the property, but you want it to be theirs.

Some might be busy, so this script below will be appropriate for such people.

Agent: *"I realize that you may be unable to speak at this time, and I am pleased to organize a callback at a convenient time. How about we arrange a callback for X time tomorrow, or if that doesn't work for you, we can find another time that does?"*

(This is to confirm their request and provide a precise time for a callback, which is usually necessary when they have a hectic schedule.)

Agent: *"I understand that you are busy, but I want to make sure that we have the time to talk about your real estate requirements. This is* *a significant decision, and I want to ensure that you have all of the information you need to make an informed decision."*

(To underline the topic's importance and remind them that the decision is critical and will necessitate a thorough discussion to facilitate decision-making.)

Agent: *"If you need to reach me before our planned callback, please see the details below. Please let me know what time works best for you, and I'll plan the callback accordingly. I hope to chat with you again soon."*

(This is where you share your contact information and ask for their desired callback time. This is your chance to motivate them to take action.)

Agent: *"Thank you for taking the time to consider me as your real estate agent. I eagerly await the opportunity to chat with you more and answer any questions you may have. Have a wonderful day, and I'll speak with you soon."*

(To conclude the talk in a positive tone.)

When scheduling a callback, remember to be flexible and accommodating. It is critical to respect the client's time and availability while also emphasizing your commitment to having a meaningful dialogue regarding their estate requirements.

96. WHAT IS YOUR COMMISSION? YOU MIGHT HAVE TO REDUCE IT.

This is where you need all the confidence you have got. You will work hard to ensure the transaction is successful with no problems, and so you deserve a fair rate. However, you must be logical about the amount you collect as a commission and ensure that it follows the real estate guidelines for your country. For example, in the United States, the commission is usually between 5 - 10 percent which the buyer and seller agents split evenly.

Real estate commission also depends on how strenuous the transaction will go, the number of homes available to you as an agent, the amount your real estate firm collects (if you are working for a firm), your years of expertise as a realtor and the antitrust laws in your country. The National Association of Realtors(NAR) recommends that a realtor should not charge less than 5%.

This script will help you understand how to state your commission to your client very convincingly.

Agent: *"Thank you for inquiring about my commission. It's a crucial factor to consider when selecting an agent, and I'm pleased to go over it with you."*

(This is to acknowledge their inquiry and thank them for their interest in your services.)

Agent: *"As a real estate agent, I get compensated based on the property's sale price. The commission is often a percentage of the selling price, distributed equally between the buyer's and seller's* *agents. In most circumstances, the seller pays the fee, although the buyer might negotiate with the seller to cover some or all of the commission."*

(This is to describe how your commission works in the simplest and most understandable way possible.)

Agent: *"My typical commission is X%, and I'm delighted to discuss this more with you. If you have a certain budget in mind, I'm also willing to look at other commission systems. We might, for example, propose a flat fee agreement or a lower commission rate. The essential thing is to discover a solution that suits you and your requirements."*

(This is to offer additional information about your unique commission structure, more like a full discussion of several commission structure choices.)

Agent: *"While it is true that employing an agent entails paying a commission, there are several advantages to doing so. An agent can save you time, stress, and money in the long run. They have access to a large number of listings and can assist you in finding the ideal house for your budget. They are also well-versed in the local real estate market and can advise you on the best bid to make and negotiate on your behalf."*

(To underline the importance of working with a real estate agent like yourself and the benefits you bring.)

When discussing your commission, remember to be open to bargaining and truthful. It's critical to underscore the importance of having an agent and how they may save the client time, worry, and possibly even money in the long run.

97. I'VE NEVER SEEN ANY OF YOUR SIGNS IN OUR NEIGHBORHOOD.

There are two answers to this, depending on if the objection is true or false. If it is false, then you are more disposed to settle the objection easily using the script below. Just ensure that you are not annoyed with this objection. In a very composed way, explain to your potential client that they are mistaken and that you have established several signs in their neighborhood. Tell him the signs and see this as a perfect opportunity to introduce yourself to them and market your properties.

If true, you must apologize for not doing that yet and thank them for bringing that to your notice. Regardless of this, introduce yourself to them and market your properties.

Here is a perfect sample script to do that.

Agent: *"Thank you for bringing this to my notice, and I'm pleased to handle your problem. It's reasonable to want to deal with an agent who knows the region well."*

(This is to appreciate their interest and thank them for inquiring about your signage in their region. That shows that they are looking forward to working with you; they only need to trust you well enough.)

Agent: *"My responsibility as a real estate agent is to advertise homes to potential buyers and sellers. To reach buyers and sellers, I employ a variety of marketing strategies, including listing properties on the MLS (multiple listing service) and other online platforms, advertising* *properties on social media and other online channels, hosting open houses and private showings for interested buyers, and finally networking with other agents and industry professionals.*

While you may not have noticed my signs in your neighborhood, I have a proven track record of success and am confident in my ability to connect you with your home's ideal buyers and sellers."

(This is majorly to discuss your marketing plan and expand on how beneficial they are even when your signs are not fully represented in their location.)

Agent: *"In addition to my marketing methods, I am intimately familiar with the local real estate market. I remain current on trends and statistics and can offer significant insights and recommendations on what to expect in the present market. This knowledge and skills, I feel, will be useful to you as we work together to buy or sell your house."*

(This is to highlight your understanding of the local market. You may say anything about how your services are well integrated with the recent updates in stats and other related updates.)

Agent: *"Based on my marketing approach and local market knowledge, I feel I am the greatest candidate to assist you in buying or selling your house. May I get the opportunity to work with you and demonstrate my worth?"*

(This is to solicit their patronage, more like a call to action to hire you as their agent.)

When responding to this objection, keep your marketing plan and understanding of the local market in mind. It's critical to demonstrate that you have a track record of success and can give the client significant insights and recommendations, even if they haven't seen your signage in their specific location.

98. WILL YOU LOWER YOUR COMMISSION IF THE OTHER AGENT DOES?

When this kind of objection surfaces, The fact is that most of the time, no additional agents are present. Prospects frequently believe they can find a cheaper agent since many people consider real estate agents a service that can be offered elsewhere for less money.

Your objective here is to change their perspective. You must demonstrate to prospects that you are not a service but an opportunity.

How are you going to go about that? This script is just right to execute that for you.

Agent: *"I believe you received an offer from another agent wanting to lower their commission. In today's market, that might be an enticing offer. However, regardless of my compensation, I want to assure you that I am devoted to providing you with the finest service possible."*

(This is to acknowledge the other agent's objection and conduct and ensure not to talk badly of the other assumed agent.)

Agent: *"While every real estate transaction includes a commission, the value of a real estate agent extends well beyond merely completing the sale. As your agent, I will work relentlessly to advertise your home, negotiate the greatest possible price, and walk you through the whole process. My objective is to ensure that you receive the greatest possible price for your home."*

(To underline the worth of your services here, you can explain how unique you are without having to feel like you overdid it because that will make you stand out, yes, your unique services.)

Agent: *"If you want, I may offer a full breakdown of the services that I will provide to you as your agent. This will assist you in making an informed decision about which agent to choose by providing a better idea of the value that I will bring to the table."*

(This is too to present a full breakdown of your services, coming down from the procedure, your marketing strategies, your negotiating skills, your connection, and most significantly, the cost that is attached to these premium services.)

Agent: *"I recognize that you have options when it comes to choosing an agent, and I would be happy to gain your business. My experience, skill, and devotion to my clients make me the greatest choice for you, in my opinion. I hope you will give me the opportunity to show it to you."*

(In this top-seller objection, you emphasize the fact that you have a vested stake in the success of a property. If another agent is ready to forego a commission in a simple chat, how would they advertise and represent their house in another? One would assume the same way.)

In most cases, an agent's commission is the primary source of income for them and their family. And while some transactions make sense, such as when a seller sells one house and buys another with the same agent, you often want to adhere to your compensation structure or provide alternate marketing packages.

For example, show them a property offered using mobile phone photos. Then show them a home professionally photographed and set by an interior designer. Ask which property they believe will attract the highest selling price. Then point out how a lower commission might limit your potential to get top cash for their property. Always remember to close the conversation with a good call to action.

99. I'M NOT SURE MY CREDIT WILL ALLOW THAT.

Some prospects want to purchase or sell but haven't gotten the correct help. Sometimes all you need to do is gently educate leads and become a part of the solution.

Here is a script to do that:

Agent: *"I strongly advise you not to give up your search for a better home due to this. I've dealt with credit repair organizations that have effectively helped my prospects improve their credit ratings."*

(This is to sympathize with them and acknowledge that you know what they are facing now and that you have experience with what can be done to solve their problem.)

Agent: *"Would you like me to ask [Company] to investigate what they can do for your credit issues?"*

(This is to provide solutions to the Clients on how they can get help with their credit issues.)

100. DISINTERESTED.

Let's be honest. Most of the time, "not interested" merely means "not interested in agents." When you discover what caused the prospect's unpleasant past experience, bring it to light and address it immediately in your presentation.

Agent: *"It sounds like you had a negative experience. Yes, for better or worse, your experience is heavily influenced by the agent with whom you deal. Do you mind me asking what the problem was?"*

(This will help you to sympathize with the client and also open a new conversation that will help you know more about the reason behind their decision at that point in time. And any Objections brought up can be resolved using one of the Scripts related to the objections we have discussed above.)

Finally, demonstrate your worth by communicating with your prospects more frequently than any other agent in your region.

101. CAN YOU REDUCE YOUR COMMISSION?

When presented with the "reduced commission" scenario, the natural reaction is establishing your value by discussing what you do and why you're worth it.

However, doing so may give the impression that you are making excuses. Instead of making the entire conversation about yourself, focus on the prospect and their main goal: saving money while working with you.

Agent: *"I appreciate your desire to save money, but let me ask you this: would you rather deal with an agent who sells your property or an agent who sells your house for the best price on the market?"*

(This is to make them think about the differences between the services you will render and that of any other agent that just wants to sell the house to get any commission from it.)

Agent: *"I'll be there for you every step of the way, ensuring you are paid fairly, but I can only do it if you trust me and understand my worth. Do you want to get the greatest price for your house?"*

(This is to let them know that all they need to do is trust you, and they will get the best price for their home and won't have to worry about the commission because they will definitely get more money from the deal than you will get them.)

102. WILL YOU REDUCE YOUR COMMISSION IF I LIST MY NEXT HOUSE WITH YOU?

As stated earlier, your commission is your asset, and this is what you live on. It would be best if you did not reduce it ridiculously to get a listing. It won't be of gain to you if you keep doing this. However you can accept minor adjustments, but it is important that your client understands the quality of your work and that you are not adjusting it because you are desperate!

Here is a lovely script that might be of help:

Agent: *"I understand you are thinking about listing your next house with me and are curious about the prospect of lowering my commission.*

I value your patronage and the opportunity to gain your confidence and loyalty. The commission is a crucial consideration in any real estate transaction, and I want to ensure that the terms of our agreement are satisfactory to you."

(To recognize the objection and the client's worry regarding the commission.)

Agent: *"As a real estate agent, I earn my commission by providing my customers with useful services and assisting them in achieving their real estate objectives. My commission is calculated as a percentage of the property's sale price and is normally paid by the seller. I would be delighted to go over my commission structure and rules with you in further depth and answer any questions you may have."*

(Here, you explain your commission structure and policies, how they work out, and why they are so.)

Agent: *"While the commission is significant, I feel that the value of a real estate agent extends much beyond a percentage of the transaction price. As your agent, I will work relentlessly to advertise your home, negotiate the greatest possible price, and walk you through the whole process. My objective is to ensure that you receive the greatest possible price for your home. I am dedicated to giving my clients the finest service possible and winning their confidence and loyalty."*

(This helps you to highlight the value of your services and your dedication to maximizing the value of their money.)

Agent: *"If the commission is a major problem for you, I am ready to discuss the idea of arranging a new agreement. However, I want to emphasize that my primary focus is on providing the best possible facility to my clients and helping them achieve their real estate goals. Please let me know if you have any further questions or concerns."*

(If required, this is to propose negotiating the commission and striking up a deal instantly; moreover, call them to act based on what you have informed them so far.)

Show your quality, and try not to sound too desperate.

103. WE HAVE AN EXCELLENT BUSINESS FRIEND.

Friendship commitments are wonderful and should be honored. However, friends might be sentimental and not as professional as they should be. Demonstrate, for example, that you can assist your prospects in obtaining the greatest potential deal by giving them comprehensive information that friends might not have the time and energy to do.

Here's a script for dealing with the objection:

Agent: *"I realize you have a close buddy in the real estate business, and it's entirely natural to want to deal with someone you know and trust. However, keep in mind that selling a property is a huge financial and emotional choice, and it is critical to find the appropriate match regarding both personal and professional compatibility."*

(This is to recognize the client's relationship with their real estate business buddy and to underline the necessity of finding the proper fit; also, you may want to tell him the possible risk of doing the latter.)

Agent: *"As a real estate agent, I have a comprehensive awareness of the local market and the needs of buyers and sellers. I have a demonstrated track record of effectively promoting and selling homes for my clients, and I think that my knowledge and ability can help you sell your house. In addition to my professional skills, I am dedicated to providing great customer service and collaborating closely with my customers to meet their requirements and goals."*

(This is to discuss the benefits of working with you above working with a friend that may seem sentimental rather than professional.)

Agent: *"I would be pleased to offer you with further information about my services and approach, I can also supply references or testimonials from former clients who can attest to the quality of care and attention I offer. I feel that hearing directly from clients who have worked with an agent is the greatest approach to appreciate the value of their services."*

(This is an invitation to share further information about your services and approach to enlighten them.)

Agent: *"I recognize you have a choice when it comes to choosing an agent, and I would be thrilled to have the opportunity to earn your business. My experience, skill, and devotion to my clients make me the greatest choice for you, in my opinion. I hope you will give me the opportunity to show it to you."*

(This is the final step of requesting the opportunity to gain their business and make them strike a deal with you.)

Friends are excellent, but they might be wrong in business transactions.

104. WILL YOU REDUCE YOUR COMMISSIONS BECAUSE OTHER AGENTS WILL IF YOU DON'T?

A typical issue with sellers is that they believe they must pay more for the agent's advice and wish to sell the property themselves. You'll need to emphasize your worth as an agent so the seller realizes they're getting exceptional service beyond the transaction!

Here's a script you may use to respond to the objection:

Agent: *"I understand you are contemplating dealing with an agent who is prepared to reduce their commission. While this may appear to be a wonderful method to save money, in order to obtain the best possible outcome, it is critical to thoroughly analyze all of the elements that might affect the sale of your house."*

(This is to address the client's worry regarding the commission and convey the value of your services.)

Agent: *"As a real estate expert, I have a thorough awareness of the local market and the needs of buyers and sellers, and I apply that knowledge to create a pricing and marketing plan targeted to your specific needs and goals. My objective is to assist you in obtaining the highest possible sale price for your house. I will do this by taking into account all aspects that are essential to you."*

(This is to describe your price and marketing strategy for the property.)

Agent: *"I have the expertise and resources you need to reach your real estate objectives as an experienced and devoted real estate agent. I have a thorough awareness of the local market and the needs of*

buyers and sellers, and I am dedicated to providing my clients with the finest service and representation available. Regardless of the commission or other fees, you may be paid. I think that my skill and devotion make me the greatest choice to help you reach your real estate goals."

(This emphasizes the importance of dealing with an experienced and professional real estate agent.)

Agent: "I would be pleased to offer you further information about my approach to pricing and promoting your home, or if you have any special issues or questions. I can also look into various solutions or tactics that might help you reach your goals while keeping your budget and limits in mind. Let's collaborate to develop a solution that matches your demands while also assisting you in achieving your real estate goals."

(This is to share additional information about your approach and to explore potential solutions.)

105. I'M GOING TO THINK ABOUT WHETHER I WANT TO WORK WITH YOU.

When a vendor suggests this to you, the last thing you want to do is be pushy or too convincing. However, because residences are frequently the most valuable asset that many sellers hold, it's fair that they want to be cautious when selecting an agent.

You may ask them,

Agent: "What is the one thing that will make you employ me on the spot today without a doubt?"

173

(This is to inquire about what they are looking for in an agent to know what aspect you need your presentation to be good at.)

Typically, they will say something indicating that they require more time.

At this stage, you should acknowledge their need for time, inform them you will be present, and demonstrate your ability to deliver value.

106. I'M BUSY AND UNABLE TO SPEAK; COULD YOU PHONE ME LATER?

The lead is simply trying to get off the phone as fast as they answered it. Whether they are brushing you off or unable to speak at that moment, you can decide whether they are worth calling back.

You want the lead to commit to a time when you can contact them back, but you also want to ensure they are selling or buying a property.

Agent: *"Just to make sure I'm not wasting your time when I call back, you're still interested in buying/selling your property, correct? Are you still seeking representation?"*

(This objection is straightforward. Simply ask the prospect if they are still interested, as people who raise this objection multiple times are unlikely to transact with you.)

CONCLUSION

Handling objections in the real estate industry can be challenging, but with the right strategies and techniques, it's possible to overcome them effectively. In this book, we have provided you with over 100 common real estate objections and their scripts and strategies to handle them. We also shared our "6 Easy Steps to Handle Any Real Estate Objections" to help you confidently approach any objection. With this vital information you are sure to be on your way to real estate success!

We hope this book will be a valuable resource moving in your real estate career. We understand that objections can be a source of frustration and stress, but by using the techniques and scripts in this book, you can turn these challenges into opportunities.

As a digital marketing expert, I believe that leveraging the power of the internet can be an effective way to generate leads and attract clients. I encourage you to visit https://SoldOutHouses.com for more resources and tools to help you grow your real estate business. Our site offers a wide range of digital marketing tools, templates, and resources to help you stand out from the competition.

Thank you for choosing this book. We hope it's been a valuable asset in your real estate career. We look forward to connecting with you again on SoldOutHouses.com for more tips, strategies, and insights.

Best regards,

Nick Tsai.

RESOURCES

Thanks for taking this book; the following are some resources that can help you take your real estate business to the next level.

1. The Ultimate Real Estate Marketing Checklist (Free)

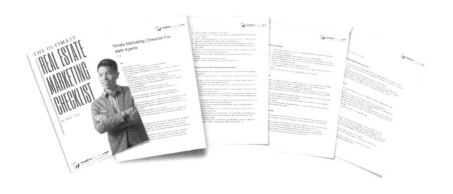

Get 86 proven real estate marketing ideas to generate more leads online.

Please go to https://soldouthouses.com/checklist to download your free checklist.

2. Sold Out Houses Pro Membership

You can also join our pro membership to get access to over 1700+ real estate marketing tools & templates for only a few bucks a day.

Go to https://soldouthouses.com/pro/
to learn more about this special package.

3. Our Digital Marketing Services

Want my team to take care of your internet marketing for you?

Visit Our site at https://services.soldouthouses.com/ to see what you can do to bring your real estate marketing to the next level.

4. 150 done-for-you real estate infographics

Get your social media content ready in the next few minutes.

You can get your infographic package at

https://soldouthouses.com/infographics.

5. 360 real estate social media post templates

Create professional social media content

quickly with those templates

You can get those templates at

https://soldouthouses.com/socialmediaposttemplates

6. 360 real estate ad templates

Create professional social media ad images
quickly with these templates.

You can get all templates at

https://soldouthouses.com/adtemplates

7. Easy Real Estate Funnels
(Done-for-you website & funnel templates)

Want to have a professional real estate website? Get our done-
for-you website and funnel template and get your website
up and running quickly.

Learn more at https://soldouthouses.com/easyfunnel

8. 10X Leadgen Masterclass

Discover how to generate more leads with digital marketing.

Sign up here at https://soldouthouses.com/masterclass

9. The Ultimate Real Estate Video Template Bundle

Get 45 Done-for-you video template for your tiktok , |
facebook and youtube marketing

Get it for a discount at

https://soldouthouses.com/videotemplates

Made in the USA
Middletown, DE
04 November 2023

41955869R00106